SEIZING
THE
MOMENT

SEIZING THE MOMENT

WARREN CURTIS-SMITH

Seizing the Moment
Published by Warren Curtis-Smith
New Zealand

© 2019 Warren Curtis-Smith

ISBN 978-0-473-49866-5 (Softcover)
ISBN 978-0-473-49867-2 (ePUB)
ISBN 978-0-473-49868-9 (Kindle)

Production & Typesetting:
Andrew Killick and Lizelle Windon
Castle Publishing Services
www.castlepublishing.co.nz

Cover design:
Paul Smith

Scripture quotations are taken from
The Authorized (King James) Version.
Rights in the Authorized Version in the United Kingdom
are vested in the Crown.
Reproduced by permission of the Crown's patentee,
Cambridge University Press.

ALL RIGHTS RESERVED

No part of this publication may be reproduced,
stored in a retrieval system, or transmitted
in any form or by any means, electronic, mechanical,
photocopying, recording or otherwise,
without prior written permission from the author.

DEDICATION

If you are a sceptic I would like to dedicate this book to you. It is okay to experience doubt in the pursuit of truth. Many criticize Jesus' disciple Thomas and have labelled him 'Doubting Thomas.' I find Thomas a valuable man in the Bible who also was a sceptic. After Jesus rose from the grave Thomas said this.

> *But Thomas, one of the twelve, called Didymus, was not with them when Jesus came* [appeared in His resurrection body from the grave].
> *The other disciples therefore said unto him, We have seen the Lord. But he said unto them, Except I shall see in his hands the print of the nails, and put my finger into the print of the nails, and thrust my hand into his side, I will not believe.*
> *And after eight days again his disciples were within, and Thomas with them: then came Jesus, the doors being shut, and stood in the midst, and said, Peace be unto you.*
> *Then said he to Thomas, Reach here thy finger, and behold my hands; and reach here thy hand, and thrust it into my side: and be not faithless, but believing.*
> *And Thomas answered and said unto him, My Lord and my God.* (John 20:24-28)

The reality of Christ's resurrection is found in the sceptic Thomas' words and reaction. When he saw Jesus, he very quickly changed his opinion and worshipped Him, calling Him his Lord and his God.

Some say that Thomas reacted out of surprise but that is not correct. His doubt became belief, he was convinced that Jesus was alive right before his eyes. This book isn't going to cause Jesus to jump off the pages, and challenge you to touch His wounds, but I hope it will prove the existence of a living, loving God who cares about you and desires for you to come to know Him if you don't already.

Warren Curtis-Smith

CONTENTS

Introduction	11
An Unusual Salvation	13
First Encounter with a Supernatural God	16
I Don't Want to Know	19
Tell the Truth	21
I Am Not Pulling Your Leg	23
The Holy Spirit Mechanic	25
The Karate Kid and the Young Reptilian	27
Your Sins Will Catch You Out	29
Making the Most of Idle Time	31
A Merry Heart Doeth Good Like a Medicine	33
Witnessing at the Checkout	35
How the Dollar Can Get You into Heaven	38
Jesus Cares About the Little Things	40
Terrorizing the Interpreter	42
The Day I Met the Man of Faith	44
How to Witness to a Legalist (Programmed Evangelist)	45
Never Too Late	48
Scary Ride to Victory	51
Deaf Mute	54
Oh Ye of Little Faith	56
Curiosity Killed the Headache	58
Transvestite Transportation Trial	59

Near Death Experience	61
Faith as Tiny as a Dot	64
When 'god' Came to Visit	66
My Son the Sunday School Apologist	69
Witnessing at a Nudist Beach	71
Shocking the Specialist	72
Generosity Missed the Point (Materialistic Mishap)	74
In the Poo More Ways Than One	76
Unwanted Resurrection	79
Abscessed Tooth	82
Another Tooth Story	84
Unsteady Sailor	85
Busy Day	87
A Little Taste of Heaven	90
Never Give Up	92
Nose Bleeder	95
Calling for Backup	96
Rapture Ready	98
Power of the Memorized Scriptures	101
Teaching My Students to Seize the Moment	103
Dangers When One Kisses a Tree Too Hard	105
Close Call	108
Ice Cream Test	110
Knocking on Heaven's Door	111
Divine Appointment	112
False Impression	114
Coven Verses Covenant	116
My Experience in a Mexican Prison	118
God's in the Room	120
Tantalizing Others with Your Testimony	122
Conclusion	124
Salvation Prayer	127

ACKNOWLEDGEMENTS

I would like to thank Bev McVicar for her great effort editing this book, as I hold no earthly qualifications in the literary field. I do however have a BA (Born again) and a PHD (Praising Him Daily) from the courts of heaven. I would also like to thank two special friends of over sixty years. Ailsa Smith and Alene Helliwell for the original grammar check.

INTRODUCTION

I would like to share some stories with you, from my life walking in the faith of the most wonderful man who ever lived. The God/Man, Yeshuah, Messiah, most commonly known as the Lord Jesus Christ. I was baptized as a baby in the Catholic Church, my Mum was a Roman Catholic. My early exposure to church was through attending the Anglican Church (Church of England), Dad was an English Catholic. My constant searching for the answers to life came to a joyous conclusion at the age of 37 when I became born again in the Baptist Church.

I came to know Jesus through the very powerful ministry of a man called Bill Subritzky. He boldly presented the gospel declaring our need for God to save us from our sinful state. This had a great impact on my life. I saw, for myself, the power of God delivering people from demonic spirits and sickness. By seeing these things with my own eyes I naturally believed that this is what we, as Christians, can and should be doing. I couldn't wait to live my life in such an exciting faith.

I loved listening to this Baptist pastor who was previously a lawyer. Christian lawyers are great teachers because they know how to present the irrefutable case for Christ and His gospel. I was now baptized in the Holy Spirit and was hungry for the things of God. I, along with my wife Pauline and our seven children, found and joined a little Assemblies of God church. Looking back at my religious life I guess you could call me a Cathanglicanbapticostalist. Pauline and I presently attend a Baptist church.

I was amazed that God could, and would, use me. I am eternally grateful to God that He reached out and grabbed me before I ended up in a lost eternity. Eternity is a long time and I was heading in the wrong direction. The only chance I had to qualify for heaven lay in the person of Jesus Christ.

I have led a very exciting life since becoming a believer in the living Lord Jesus. Additionally experiencing the baptism of the Holy Spirit has set me on an amazing adventure. I believe God speaks to us through His word and I have a passion for the truths found in the Bible. I hope you find my eye witness accounts uplifting and encouraging. My hope is that you discover Jesus through these words, and that your faith is increased as we exalt Him. Together let's bask in His wonderful ability to do things way beyond our capabilities to the point where we just have to stand back and say WOW!

| AN UNUSUAL SALVATION

When I was in my twenties I had that constant niggle about the reason for life and the question, "Why am I here?" In hindsight I can see that, right from a young child, God had His finger on me. Even though my brother and I swore a lot neither of us could tolerate other people using the Lord's name in vain. For years I searched, delving into ESP, UFOs etc. but it wasn't until I was thirty-seven before I became a devoted follower of Christ.

Pauline (my wife) and I would bundle up the kids and go to church every now and again thinking that it was good to get on the right side of God. One morning a member of the church announced that there was an evangelical outreach coming to town and they needed counsellors for the meeting. Being country folk, and by definition always happy to help out, we put our hands up to volunteer. We were instructed to attend a training evening with a video produced by the said evangelist. This was a good idea as it gave everyone the understanding of how he wanted people to minister after the meeting. Pauline and I sat there listening to the pastor who was running the meeting and then he said something that gripped my soul.

"If there is any unconfessed sin in your life why not come to the front. We will pray with you and that way our training starts out with us being right with the Lord," or words to that effect. I knew right away I had a problem that made me feel very guilty; something Pauline did not know about.

I had led my wife to believe, for the previous few months, that I had quit smoking. Although I had cut back considerably I still had a stash of cigarettes, strategically planted around our property, so I could have a sneaky smoke every now and then. I felt so bad when we visited friends and Pauline would tell them of my wonderful achievement – knocking off smoking. Next thing I knew I was up the front telling the pastor I had a problem not being able to quit smoking. He said, "Repeat after me: 'Dear Lord I renounce this cigarette smoking and repent of it in the name of Jesus.'"

I think the word repent opened the door that gave Jesus access into my life. I then experienced an amazing fragrance accompanied by a breeze which brushed past me. Incredibly I burst out in a strange language and the rest, as they say, is history. I had now become, what is known as, born again.

I'm not saying that this is the way it is supposed to happen, it is however, my experience. Nobody knew that I was not already a born-again believer and we carried on with the video. Pauline received Jesus as her Saviour that night as well which was great as we were born again on the same day.

The visiting evangelist was Bill Subritzky who moved in signs and wonders. After the altar call, and in the rooms at the back of the venue, there was ministry for the new believers. Pauline and I thought that the room set aside for deliverance from demonic spirits would be the place to be, so we volunteered for that. Nobody questioned how long we had been Christians so we were accepted to be counsellors and slotted into the deliverance ministry.

The big night came and Counsellor Warren and Counsellor Pauline had no idea what they were in for. I remember listening to this Subritzky guy who could really preach up some fire and brimstone to the point where I could feel myself sinking into the flames of hell. I think I was physically sinking further and further down in my seat when I heard God speak to me. It wasn't an audible voice but more like an inner voice and He said. "It's okay, you're saved." I will never forget the wonderful feeling that came with that simple phrase and I was never the same again. I was, as the Bible puts it, a new creation in Christ Jesus. From the time I confessed my addiction to cigarettes I never have had a desire or craving to smoke again. I thank God for healing me. I was such a heavy smoker I doubt, that without God's intervention, I would have survived as long as I have. How could I not follow such a wonderful loving God.

FIRST ENCOUNTER WITH A SUPERNATURAL GOD

From a very young age I knew I wanted to be a farmer. When I was five I wanted to be a poultry farmer. I would spend every spring afternoon, on my way home from school, gazing in the window at the day old chicks in my uncle's hardware store. He knew I loved these little fluffy chicks and he would give me the sick chickens to take home to try and nurse back to health. I had quite a good success rate. I cut strips out of an old woollen cardigan and hung them over a board to mimic the feathers of a mother hen. I would put the chickens in the box and they would climb under this strange new mum. I then added the critical ingredient of warmth by putting the box into the hot water cupboard.

Despite my early success with the chickens, I later decided to be a pig farmer and was quite excited about that until I went to stay on my uncle's dairy farm. My uncle was my hero, a big jolly man who loved life with a passion. Everything in his world that could be made into some kind of competition became a race. First thing in the morning at 5:00 a.m. he would let his three-legged dog 'Wag' go to round up the milking herd. The race began as soon as the dog was let loose. We would jump in his little Morris Minor and back slowly down the drive, as the race had to be fair. Then he would drive down the hill to the end of the farm and we would jump out and listen in the dark to see if the dog was already there.

First Encounter with a Supernatural God

If Wag could be heard rounding up the cows my uncle would be elated on how fast that three-legged dog could run.

My uncle's cowshed was called a walkthrough and the cows would head for their preferred milking bail. He knew them each one and all and, most importantly, he managed to be "out of the firing line" when putting on the cups. Even this feat was turned into a performance. He would make me a milo (chocolate drink) from the nice warm milk fresh from the cows and when I was distracted he would pull the cow's teat and squirt me with milk. I loved this great big 6ft 5in man so full of life. Then the dreaded reality of farming life hit home. In those days the milk was put through a separator to separate the milk from the cream. The cream went into a cream can and was trolleyed out to the road to be picked up by the cream lorry. The skim milk was pumped to the pig shed to feed the pigs. The shed had a low roof to keep in the warmth but it also kept in the smell. It was time to clean out the pig shed. The smell was absolutely unbelievable so my uncle had a wonderful plan to make this hellish task more palatable.

I was twelve years old and both my father and uncle smoked. I knew it was forbidden for me until I was at least sixteen although this didn't stop the longing I had to pass through this rite of passage into manhood. My uncle knew the task needed some compromise to get me to even enter that hell hole of stench. Disregarding the niceties of the law, he rolled me a smoke and one for himself then said. "This will help boy, when it's lit dive in and start scraping." I was willing to suffer the stench spurred on by the thought that I was just like my uncle with the bonus of smoking and not getting in trouble. The downside was that set me up with such a love for the smell of tobacco smoke that I became addicted.

When I left school, I started work on a large dairy farm getting up at 3:45 a.m. to milk and finishing work at 6:30 p.m. This regime was quite a shock to my system. After four years learning the ropes of dairy farming and two years shearing sheep I was able to get a Rural Bank loan to purchase a herd of cows. I got a share milking job and was very excited to have my own cows. I anticipated that if things went well I would, within a few years, have the deposit for a farm.

The farmer I was share milking for had just purchased the farm and, to quickly increase pasture levels, he had put a large amount of fertilizer on the land. The resultant lush grass can be fatal for cows as it can produce a gaseous build up in their stomach. If they are unable to burp out this gas the pressure can increase until it crushes their heart and they die. This can happen quite suddenly and a farmer stands to lose a lot of cows if they can't be treated quickly with anti-bloat drench. As a last resort the gas could be released by stabbing the cow in the top of the stomach. Cows who had this treatment seldom recovered to full health. Each night after milking I would check the cows for bloat.

One evening I checked and to my horror all I could see was badly bloated cows. They were too bloated to be moved as that would have made them worse. I was afraid I was going to lose most of my cows and that would have meant financial ruin. In desperation I knelt down and prayed for God to help me. At that time of my life I didn't pray at all, I didn't even give God much of my time if any, but I was desperate. All of a sudden while my head was bowed, I noticed an incredible stillness came over the whole paddock. The birds stopped their evening singing and it was dead still. I lifted my eyes and discovered that all the cows were fine with no sign of bloat anywhere. It is undeniable that I had witnessed a miracle, sadly though, it was some years later before I surrendered my life to the Lord. However, my God is an awesome God and I am so grateful He never gave up on me.

I DON'T WANT TO KNOW

While out, beating my feet around a country town in Northland New Zealand, knocking on doors hoping to get a carpet cleaning job, I came across a chap who was a socialist atheist. There was no way I would be getting the chance to clean his carpet so after a quick try at sharing the gospel I moved on and managed to get a job right across the cul-de-sac.

The guy, whose carpet I was cleaning, was a bachelor and I prayed for God to give me an opportunity to tell him about Jesus. On finishing the job I had a strong feeling that he had a sore back. Do you have a sore back? I asked and he said yes. I boldly declared he had one leg shorter than the other and if he could put on a nice pair of shoes, I would check him out. As he sat in the middle of his kitchen with his legs straight out in front of him, I could see a difference of a good half inch. I asked if he could see the difference and he said that he couldn't. I thought, "This is no good we need a witness to God's goodness."

Just then there was a knock at the door and I saw the head of the socialist atheist appear at the door. I immediately said, "You are just the man I need. Can you see that one leg is shorter than the other?"

He said, "Yeah."

I said, "God is going to make them the same length watch this."

As I prayed from a distance the man's leg grew out to be the same length as the other one. I looked toward the door to catch the atheist's reaction but he had gone. Not long after there was another knock at the door. This time the man's neighbour came in and wanted to know what was going on. He said that George (the socialist atheist, not his real name) went running over to his house holding his ears and yelling, "I don't want to know, I don't want to know." I hope and pray that George did come to know the Creator and believe there is a God and His Son's name is Jesus.

TELL THE TRUTH

The mission I was directing in the Philippines taught weekly values classes at the local high school. This was voluntary work throughout all the schools in the Philippines incorporating wonderful lessons on good morals. I was assisting a younger colleague and I could see that the class of sixty students weren't paying attention. There was just one ceiling fan in the room; not a good environment to get brain cells operating in tropical heat. I thought to myself, I will give them a quick lesson on good morals. I wrote on the blackboard without saying a thing, "Who wants 10,000 pesos?" ($300). I immediately had their attention. I then said if you can tell me you have never sinned you can have it. Immediately there was a big sigh from the class. Now that I had their attention, I thought it best to try and keep it.

I then wrote on the board, "40,000 pesos. Who wants 40,000 pesos?" and of course, everyone would like that much cash. This offer was met with a bit less enthusiasm as they thought I might catch them out again. I then said, "If you can find this place mentioned in the Bible, I will give you 40,000 pesos." I then wrote in big letters PURGATORY across the blackboard. I cautioned, "Don't you tell others that I said it wasn't in the Bible, but if you can find it, I will give you 40,000 pesos." A young man, who had been wrestling with consciousness in the twilight zone, suddenly was fully alert and asked me how I was going to pay him. I assured him that if he could find it, I would pay him.

Two weeks went by without any news so I wrote on the board: "40,000 pesos".

The whole class shouted, "Purgatory, wala, wala." ("Nothing, nothing".) I figured that they hadn't all read the Bible from one end to the other in two weeks, but had paid a visit to Mr. Google at the local internet café. That was a simple Bible lesson on the importance of truth and a group of girls from the class joined our after-school Bible studies.

> *Beware lest any man spoil you through philosophy and vain deceit, after the tradition of men* [extra biblical religious ideas]*, after the rudiments of the world, and not after Christ.* (Colossians 2:8)

I AM NOT PULLING YOUR LEG

While Pauline and I were working with church youth, I had to make extra income as I was only employed part time. I would carry a Kirby vacuum cleaner on my shoulder and knock on doors hoping for work. The machine was so powerful it would almost suck up the floor boards.

One day I got to deep clean and shampoo the lounge room of a young lady who had one leg about four inches shorter than the other. She said it was very tiring and that she would have to rest after walking only for ten minutes. Being full of faith I told her that God could heal her. I got her to sit on a chair in her dining room with her legs out straight in front of her. Being alone in the house with her, I thought it wise to not lay hands on her to pray. I stood back and prayed that God would make her legs the same length. I said you just watch and went out in the lounge and carried on cleaning. All of a sudden the lady screamed.

I said, "What happened?"

She had not fallen off the chair but replied, "My leg just shot out an inch."

"That's great," I said, "keep watching," and after three or four squeals of amazement from the dining room God had made both her legs the same length.

I have heard of faith healers (one of which I am not) playing tricks by pulling the sole of the shoe out to line up with the other

Seizing the Moment

shoe as they pray. I feel saddened that people would do such things and I hope that this story will restore faith to those who have had their leg pulled in the past.

THE HOLY SPIRIT MECHANIC

I would like to share a story that took place when Pauline and I were leading the Whangarei Assemblies of God youth group in the late 80s and early 90s. One rainy night there was a knock on my door. I opened the door and I was looking at a man soaking wet and asking for help to fix his car that had broken down in our driveway. He asked me if I knew anything about car engines. As I felt I was representing the Kiwi blokes in the world, I had no excuse but to say, "I know a bit." Then I followed him out into the rain to help him. They say that going to McDonalds doesn't turn you into a hamburger or going to church won't make you a Christian. My father was an A Grade mechanic but that never made me one.

I looked under the hood and couldn't see anything obvious as he tried to start the engine several times. I didn't fancy getting wet and cold working on his car especially when I didn't have clue where to start. I decided to tell the man I was a Christian and believed God could fix the problem. I had heard of a Baptist pastor from Tauranga who travelled the country preaching the gospel. He had an old bomb of a car that would only start if he anointed it using the oil on the dipstick. I removed the dip stick and anointed the engine with the oil on the stick in the name of the Father, Son and Holy Ghost. Replacing the dip stick, I said, "Okay, try it again." Of course, the engine burst into life! The man, full of appreciation, drove away.

The next day he was back on my doorstep with 10 cans of beer, looking so thankful he offered them to me. He said he was sorry it wasn't a full dozen but he had already drunk a couple of the cans. He asked, "You do drink?"

I said I did (I did drink but only water and other non-alcoholic beverages) and thanked him for the beer and that it was not necessary. Being a good Pentecostal I put the tray of beer under our bed and forgot about it.

Months later we were sent out by our church to pioneer a new work in Auckland. We had the youth group come and help us pack the furniture van and I asked the guys if they could get our bed. When they lifted up the bed, lo and behold there was the tray of beer that I had forgotten about with two cans missing. Talk about a jaw dropping moment as they looked surprised, confused and shocked all at the same time. They almost dropped the bed, and, feeling like a right twit, I was about to try and explain the situation when I thought I'd best let things lie. I doubted they would have believed my story about how the beer got there.

THE KARATE KID AND THE YOUNG REPTILIAN

One Sunday evening service in the 90s I was ministering prayer after the service when I noticed an elder of our church praying for a young man around 20 years old. All of a sudden, the young man flared up into a Karate strike position. The elder was a slightly built man and, being busy praying, he had not noticed what was happening. I saw that as the young man tried to strike the elder, he froze solid and was unable to move. I walked over and picked him up and to my surprise he remained totally rigid. I quickly carried him out the door of the hall with his angry snarling contorted facial expression and arm up in the strike position. I wanted to get him away from the crowd so the demon could not show-off. I placed him down and said, "Get out in Jesus' name."
Immediately he was released of the evil spirit and hugged me saying, "That's better, thanks bro."

As I was walking back into the meeting a young teenage boy (a friend of the Karate Kid) asked me if I would bless him. I sensed that he had seen the power of God working and that his focus was on me instead of on the Lord Jesus.

I said to the young man, "If you can say to me, 'Jesus is my Lord,' I will bless you."

As he went to speak the words his throat locked up as if he was being strangled. Once again he tried to say the words and again something unseen grabbed his throat. The third time he tried he slid down the wall and began writhing around on the floor. I grabbed his arm to help him up and his skin felt cold and leathery. He was not in the mood to receive Christ as his Saviour and so he became the Karate Kid's first assignment.

| YOUR SINS WILL CATCH YOU OUT

My older brother and I endured religious classes after school to prepare us for the Anglican tradition of 'Confirmation' where the Bishop laid hands on us. We were now allowed to 'take' Holy Communion. This meant we could eat the wafer and drink (sip) the wine. One of the congregation was a man who my brother and I really admired. He was a hard-working man with a lovely family. He worked as a fencer and was physically very strong. We also knew he had a liking for the taste of the communion wine. The vicar also knew this and when it was time for communion he would prepare himself for the battle ahead.

When the cup was offered to Tom he would hold the base of the goblet and lift the cup to get a swig almost lifting the vicar off the ground, as he fought to keep the cup from being emptied. Tom always managed to get a good swig. That meant if my brother and I wanted any we needed to be ahead of him in the line.

I had very little understanding of what Church and Communion was all about (perhaps if I had taken more notice of the lessons I might have). We knew if the minister was in good form, he could rattle through the service in fifty minutes. We would sit at the back of the church and time him, and then we would make a dash for the door as soon as the final benediction was said.

On our way home, we would stop off at the local milkman's garage where he parked his little Ford Thames milk truck. Perched invitingly on a ledge on the back wall was a bottle of wine labelled 'Happy Days'. We could have a good swig without raising suspicion because Mum would just think it was the smell of communion wine. We also considered it was Tom's fault as we never got a proper sip during the service.

The Exclusive Brethren church was just a stone's throw away from the milkman's garage and I mean it really was just a literal stone's throw. That gave us the idea to throw a stone onto the roof of the church then hide back in the garage and watch if there was any reaction to the sound of the stone rolling down the tin roof of the church. Two elders came out and looked around and went back inside.

I still remember that wine and the sneaky delight we experienced until one day the shiny bald head of the milkman came around the corner and caught us red handed. "Gotcha, you little b*%##s," he growled and sent us home with a stern warning.

| MAKING THE MOST OF IDLE TIME

One day while shopping in a mall in Manila with my wife I waited patiently as she tried on some tops. I had learnt over the years that shopping is far more than meets the eye for women. For most guys shopping is similar to hunting. You see it, you shoot it, you bag it and take it home. For most women looking must be followed by touching then touching is followed by some type of bonding by gently rubbing the material and stroking the arm of the garment before moving onto the next one that might catch their eye. This process can take some time. By the way I am blessed with a thrifty wife who is very wise with money so on this occasion she must have found something really worthwhile.

I started a conversation with the young man at the counter and said in my New Zealand accent, "How are you today?"

The young man looked very concerned and replied, "I don't want to die!"

I knew that my accent was the problem and he thought I had said, "How are you to die?" I realized I had been given a moment to seize and never apologized for my terrible accent. I asked, "Don't you know where you are going when you die?"

He said he didn't.

I said he had the choice of two places and one was way better than the other.

He said he didn't believe in hell.

I looked at him really concerned and scratching my head I said, "Do you think Jesus got it wrong?"

He said, "Oh no I don't think Jesus would get it wrong."

I asked him if he thought Jesus would lie.

He said no he didn't think Jesus would lie.

I told him that Jesus spoke of hell more than heaven and if He said it was real, as He is the way, the truth and the life, it must be true.

He thought about it and agreed to change his mind and I had the privilege of praying with him and leading him to Jesus. I quickly went down to the next floor to a book shop and bought the young man a Bible. I will always remember the smile on his face as he experienced the saving grace of a God who loved him. As for this "mere male" I can't remember if Pauline bought the top or not.

A MERRY HEART DOETH GOOD LIKE A MEDICINE

I am a musician and enjoy putting Christian lyrics to secular songs. One night I was asked to play for a prayer meeting. This was new to me and I wondered how it would go. I had heard in music seminars how some music is really anointed, I would not have put my music in that category. A small group arrived and we gathered in the lounge and I began to play one of my rearranged songs. The opening number was 'Faith in God' that went to Elvis Presley's 'Blue Suede Shoes'. When I finished the group burst into prayer. They were wonderful prayers and they really put their hearts into it. As the praying would die down I would play another song, this time it was the Bee Gees tune 'Staying Alive' which I changed to 'He's Alive' and when I finished the same thing happened. This prayer meeting was the strangest one I had ever been to and also one of the most enjoyable.

The next night at church an elderly lady, who was at the prayer meeting with her husband, approached me. She came to tell me that her husband, who had suffered from depression for years, had been set free through the music during the prayer meeting.

Another time I played my version of 'Amazing Grace' to a reggae beat and I witnessed two spirits at work in the church. One of the long-time members was so upset that I would play such an evil sound in a church building he refused to remain in the church and stormed out. When I finished the song I gave a call for salvations and a lady came to the front and gave her heart to the Lord. The legalistic man who had earlier left the building missed the blessing completely.

Music is a powerful medium, and just as happy and uplifting music can bring hope and healing, some music can bring a spirit of depression and death. Sadly, the music and lyrics many young ones listen to is like poison to their souls. I believe happiness and joy that reaches deep into our soul does act like a medicine, just as the Bible says.

> *A merry heart doeth good like a medicine: but a broken spirit drieth the bones.* (Proverbs 17:22)

There is no such thing as an evil note but music is affected by the spirit from where it originates.

After singing my original song called 'Almost Stoned' (the Bible story about the woman caught in adultery) a woman came forward and asked for prayer to set her free from the lifestyle she knew was not pleasing to the Lord. Nobody asked her to do that, she was responding to the song. Music is a wonderful thing and I thank God for the gift He has given me.

It is interesting when we understand that angels are never recorded in the bible as singing. The saints are seen in heaven singing. The reason is that the angels do not understand redemption because they have not experienced it and never will. Only redeemed sinners can understand what it means to be saved from their sins and from an eternal hell. God loves to hear the worship songs of the saints because they understand His kindness and grace towards them.

WITNESSING AT THE CHECKOUT

In the 90s I was standing at a checkout in a store that had the scanner on a flexible lead. As the lady placed the last items in my shopping bag I reached over and grabbed the scanner. I waved it across my forehead while looking intensely at the computer screen. As she turned around, she saw what I was doing.

I said, "Oh, you haven't got the technology yet? Perhaps you will have soon."

She then said with a slightly panicky voice, "I used to go to church and I heard about that."

I said, "You need to go back again, Jesus is coming soon. Have a nice day."

It is interesting to see how far that technology has advanced in recent years. Thousands in Sweden and many around the world have already had the microchip implanted in their hand. Many don't realize the danger of such a system which puts control of the masses in the hands of an elite few. For instance if there is no longer any cash being used, and you are out of favour, they can just switch off your chip and there is nothing you can do about it. The following verses from the Bible are to be understood as a warning from a loving Father.

And I beheld another beast [this is the False Prophet, the religious leader] *coming up out of the earth; and he had two horns like a lamb, and he spoke as a dragon.*

And he exercises all the power of the first beast [this is the Antichrist] *before him, and causes the earth and them which dwell therein to worship the first beast, whose deadly wound was healed.* [Most likely a clone of the Antichrist will be killed, then after a few days the real one will emerge as if he has resurrected from the dead.]

And he doeth great wonders, so that he makes fire come down from heaven on the earth in the sight of men,

And deceives them that dwell on the earth by the means of those miracles which he had power to do in the sight of the beast; saying to them that dwell on the earth, that they should make an image to the beast, which had the wound by a sword, and did live.

And he had power to give life unto the image of the beast, that the image of the beast should both speak, and cause that as many as would not worship the image of the beast should be killed.

And he causes all, both small and great, rich and poor, free and bond, to receive a mark in their right hand, or in their foreheads:

And that no man might buy or sell, save he that had the mark, or the name of the beast, or the number of his name.

Here is wisdom. Let him that hath understanding count the number of the beast: for it is the number of a man; and his number is Six hundred threescore and six. (Revelation 13:11-18)

This passage of scripture does not give one the warm fuzzies. However, we can learn a lot from history.

- When Noah built a great big rectangle box on dry land that was to float, full of every kind of animal the people must have thought he had lost his mind.

- When Jeremiah warned the people if they didn't change their evil lifestyle they would be taken away by the Babylonians. They tied him in the stocks, put him in prison and threw him down a well. Pessimism is not what makes one popular.
- A prophet called Macaiah in the time of Israel's kings told the wicked king Ahab that he would be killed in battle against the Syrians. He was hated for his gloomy prophecy.

All these predictions came to pass because God's word is true and optimism or pessimism have nothing to do with the warnings from our heavenly Father who offers us truth and the way of hope. The world on the other hand offers us manmade solutions for trying to cope in a world under crisis management.

HOW THE DOLLAR CAN GET YOU INTO HEAVEN

I was repairing the deck at the house we were renting to lovely people with a teenage son called Whitu. He was a likable young man and was very willing to help so I let him hammer in some nails. He showed good work skills and he really impressed me. As we chatted, I pulled my wallet from my pocket and opening it I took out an American dollar bill. I began to show Whitu the satanic symbols on the back of the dollar and what they represented to the secretive ones who put them there. He was fascinated by this and soon I was able to show him how the pyramid declared a coming new world order. I told him what the Bible had to say about this one world government system. It wasn't long and Whitu was very keen to ask Jesus into his heart. We prayed together and when we finished praying, he said he felt lighter. He experienced a real life changing moment as he was born again.

On my way home I stopped off at the church to see if they had any Bibles to give away so I could take one back the next day for Whitu. The pastor's wife was there and she said they had some NIVs that had been left in the church and never claimed.

Being prompted by my stirring nature, I said, "Those are Jehovah's Witness Bibles, aren't they?"

"What do you mean?" she said.

I said, "It was written using the same manuscripts and they have left a whole lot of stuff out." I suggested she find Acts 8:37.

How the Dollar Can Get You into Heaven

She looked it up but something was horribly wrong. The number for the verse was there but there was no verse. Shocked and bewildered she said, "I have an NIV in my office I will check it out." She rushed off to her office and soon I heard a cry of unbelief. "What, how dare they!" I took the Bible and said it will do for a starter as it is easy to read.

Whitu was grateful for the Bible and I encouraged him to get a job and it wasn't long before he was doing well working at the local community youth centre. Everyone there loved Whitu and what is really cool, is that Whitu came to Christ through the back of a dollar bill.

JESUS CARES ABOUT THE LITTLE THINGS

While I was training to become a pastor a lady from our church brought her friend along to see me. She told me that her friend could do with a miracle. Her friend told me of her situation; She had cancer in her third vertebrae. She had recently gone to see her specialist and driven two hours to get there. After taking an x-ray the doctor asked her how she had got there. She told him she had driven down. He then said it was lucky she didn't have to brake suddenly as if she had her neck would have broken. Wow! What a story. I began to tell her about Jesus and how much he loved her.

As I was chatting with her, I had a strange thought. I told her that I had a picture in my mind of Jesus preparing her home in heaven and that he was putting up some wallpaper. As I'm saying this I'm thinking to myself, "What are you doing?" I have learnt that sometimes you just have to go with it. I carried on and told her the pattern and colour of the wallpaper. She was very receptive to what I told her next. "You need to give your life over to Jesus, because He cares about you." She immediately received Jesus as her Saviour and they left.

The next Sunday at church the lady who brought her came up to me and told me what had happened with her friend. She said that when I told her about Jesus putting up the wallpaper, I had her attention but when I described the pattern, she was convinced Jesus loved and cared about her. The wallpaper was the same as the one she had chosen and was to be put in her lounge and she knew she was not going to live long enough to see it on the wall. Jesus is amazing!

Let not your heart be troubled: ye believe in God, believe also in me.

In my Father's house are many mansions: if it were not so, I would have told you. I go to prepare a place for you. (John 14:1-2)

TERRORIZING THE INTERPRETER

In 2002 Pauline and I were taking a Youth with a Mission (YWAM) team on outreach in Mexico. I had been asked to preach in a fairly large church and while I waited for the service to begin, I decided to ask the Lord if there were any special needs for prayer. I felt my hand go to the area behind my right ear. I sensed that someone there had a problem just behind their right ear. I continued to pray but nothing else came to mind. I went forward to preach and met my interpreter, a young Mexican woman, who appeared to be very nervous. Being new to the international preaching scene, and having no experience using an interpreter, I carried on in my New Zealand accent, unaware of the amount of slang that was flowing out of my mouth, and the speed of which we Kiwis (New Zealanders) speak.

The young girl struggled along for some time trying to make sense of what I was saying. I said something that she had just a vague idea of what I was getting at and asked me, "Does that mean such and such?"

I replied, "Giveitashot."

Terror gripped the young woman's face and she ran from the stage asking another person to try and understand this weird New Zealander. We did manage to get to the end of my message and I was relieved to be able to go back to my seat. However, God had not finished with me yet (He is so patient).

As my foot stepped off the stage, I remembered what He had

shown me before the service. I was not feeling very full of faith after my botched attempt at preaching to 600 amigos with a broad Kiwi accent. I stopped and said, "God wants to heal somebody who has something wrong behind their right ear." All of a sudden over in the corner of the church near the front people began to jump and clap and praise the Lord. They brought one of their group, a man, forward for prayer. When he got to me, I could see he was in a bad way. His breath smelt so bad it was hard not to throw up. His head was incredibly swollen behind his right ear and when I put my hand on it, it was really hot and hard. The poor guy was obviously in pain.

I prayed now with renewed faith as I knew it wasn't my imagination playing tricks on me before the service but rather it was the Lord guiding me (what a buzz). When I finished praying for him, I believed that when I took my hand away his neck would be back to normal. However, that was not to be. Many times things don't happen the way we think they will. The pastors of the church were encouraged when they saw that God had singled this man out. They escorted him to a room to the side and continued to pray for the man and lo and behold the massive swelling began to shrink.

God's ways are higher and different than ours, and it sure is fun being in the mix of it.

THE DAY I MET THE MAN OF FAITH

I have noticed that often nonbelievers, when questioning your beliefs, will fire their best shot first. I pulled into a service station to fill up my van with petrol and a young attendant came up to me as I was about to climb out. Noticing my Bible on the passenger's seat and before he even said hello, he said to me, "I don't believe in that stuff."

I asked him, "What stuff?"

He said, "All that God stuff."

I was quite taken aback by his boldness in making such a declaration of his beliefs. As I climbed out, I put on my confused look. I said to him, "I look around and see the trees, birds, flowers and I just believe God made it all and I am very pleased to meet you." As I shook his hand I said, "I have never met a man with so much faith."

I headed for the counter to pay my bill. On returning to my van I noticed the young man staring into the sky in a kind of dreamy like state.

As I went to get in my van, he called to me, "You know what? Maybe I do believe in God."

I gave him a grin and as I drove off, I noticed he was still pondering this new line of thought. I guess his big shot kind of ricocheted and came back to bite him in a nice way.

HOW TO WITNESS TO A LEGALIST (PROGRAMMED EVANGELIST)

A wonderful friend of mine was a born evangelist or should I say a born-again evangelist, actually he was both. He loved witnessing for Christ and like a good evangelist was always looking for a moment to seize to spread the good news of Jesus. He tells the story of travelling overseas and sitting next to a young man on the plane. After some small talk the young man broke out with his rehearsed witnessing plan, with the hope of leading my friend to the Lord.

My friend knew right away where he was going with this questioning and just played along. The young man began his practiced routine of questioning and asked him if he had ever told a lie? He said yes, he had. He asked him if he had ever taken something that didn't belong to him. He said yes, he had. He then asked him the big one, if he had ever looked at a woman lustfully. My friend said yes, he had. The young man had now presented his case and was now about to proceed with the judgement section of his presentation.

He said to my friend, "According to your own words and the words of the holy scriptures you are a lying, thieving adulterer." In the mind of the young man his hope was that this statement would bring my friend to an awareness of his filthy state before a holy God and basically plead with him to receive salvation.

Without as much as a 'how do you do' my friend said, "I don't believe that. I believe I was a dog in a past life."

Now my friend was about to find out that this young man had a great knowledge on reincarnation and the evils of it. After a lengthy lecture on the dangers of such a belief my friend once again said, "No, I don't believe that. I was a dog in a past life. In fact, I will tell you how I know."

My friend then began to tell him his story.

"One day I was running around my lawn when I felt the urge to you know? That's what dogs do when you let them out to run around. Well I liked the family that fed me so I thought it more respectful to pooh on the neighbour's lawn. I ran across the road and left my deposit on their lawn. On my way back across the road it happened, I was run over by a car. It ran right over my neck and broke it. If you don't believe me, put your hand on the back of my neck you can feel the bump where the car hit me."

As the young man reached out and felt the back of his neck my friend swung round and barked and snarled in his face. This brought the conversation to another level.

My friend then introduced himself and said that he too was an evangelist. He said that there are many different ways to present the gospel and the importance of working in partnership with the Holy Spirit, and how pre-planned strategies can be limiting and not as successful as one may have been led to believe. Such strategies may have worked in the 1800s, but that doesn't mean they are guaranteed to do so in the 21st century.

There are many ways to present the gospel but there is only one way to salvation. In our so-called progressive world this statement is often shunned because it seems too narrow. It wasn't Christians who first said there is only one way to the Father but, Jesus Himself.

I am the way, the truth and the life, no man/woman comes unto the Father but through Me. (John 14:6)

The word 'way' in this verse is singular, just the one way and, Jesus is the only way (despite what Oprah Winfrey says).

NEVER TOO LATE

While trying to pioneer a church on the North Shore of Auckland NZ I received a call from one of my congregation. She was a nurse and was passing by one of the private wards where a man was dying of stomach cancer. He was in a real bad way with not many days left to live.

She called me to ask if I would go to the city and visit as he had reluctantly agreed to see me (she was a very persuasive person). She said members of his family had tried to share their faith with him but he seemed shut off to their efforts. This is often the case with those who are close like family and friends. I agreed to go, and travelled over that night to see him. I arrived at his room but he had many family visitors who had come to say their goodbyes. I waited in the hall and spent the time reminding God that I had no idea what I was going to say to this poor man, and I would really appreciate all the help He could give me.

Finally, the visitors left and I was allowed in. Only the man and his wife were in the room. Not knowing him from a bar of soap I walked up to his bed and held out my hand and introduced myself. I then went straight to the scriptures. "I would like to read this from the Bible to you:"

> *Let not your heart be troubled: ye believe in God, believe also in me.*

> *In my Father's house are many mansions: if it were not so, I would have told you. I go to prepare a place for you.*
>
> *And if I go and prepare a place for you, I will come again, and receive you unto myself; that where I am, there ye may be also.*
>
> *And whither I go ye know, and the way ye know.*
>
> *Thomas said unto him, Lord, we know not where thou goes; and how can we know the way?*
>
> *Jesus said unto him, I am the way, the truth, and the life: no man comes unto the Father, but by me.* (John 14:1-6)

I then said, "That's the deal! Do you want to take it or not?"

He said, "I'll take it."

We prayed together and he gave his life over to Christ his newfound Saviour. He was very sincere as he prayed wanting to get it right. I was making it up as I went along (as long as you cover the main points of salvation that's okay). He was struggling to pray through the effects of the drugs that were reducing his suffering and said, "Can you repeat that again please?"

I had forgotten what I said, so quickly went over that part of the prayer again hoping any variances in my first version wouldn't throw him off track. He had been brought up in a church where all the prayers are read out of a book. We both got through the prayer and the Holy Spirit paid him a visit. He was blessed with a peace he had never experienced in his life before.

His wife was watching this unfold before her eyes so I asked her if she loved him. She said she did. I then said, "If you want to see him again you need to give your life to Jesus as well."

She agreed and so we prayed together and she too became a born again believer. As they cuddled each other I slipped out the door.

At that time I was trying to pioneer a church with my wife and I didn't think I was doing that great. On the way home the events of the past few hours were on my mind. This man was not receptive to members of his family who were more experienced pastors so why did he listen to me? I went to the source of all truth, and asked the Lord, "What has just happened?"

I quickly received in my spirit, "He's a businessman." What had happened was that God answered my desperate prayer in the hall before I went into his room. I needed God to help me. Then I realized why I had been so abrupt and went straight into reading God's word. He didn't know me and I didn't know him but God knew the exact words in the scriptures that would speak to his heart. He was a big-time businessman with an international company and was used to doing deals. People like that want to get straight to the point of the deal. I had said those exact words when I spoke to him and offered to him the deal of all deals, and he took it.

It is from this and other experiences I know it is a must to realize that we can do nothing without God's help. Whatever we get to do for the Lord should be seen as shining the glory back to God as we get to see Him at work in our life and the lives of others. This sure is an exciting ride.

SCARY RIDE TO VICTORY

I had the opportunity to travel to a very remote village in the Philippines to do a medical and dental outreach. The village was on the east coast of the island of Luzon. To get there we travelled by bus across some narrow mountainous roads. Now I have a fear of heights and sitting on the outside seats looking down the steep sides of the mountain was frightening. I am sure the driver of the bus believed he was a rally car driver because he was throwing the bus around every corner as if there was no tomorrow. I remember looking out the window and seeing a fissure in the road right on the edge, thinking if I feel the bus bump over that crack in the road this guy is driving right on the edge of the cliff. Guess what? I felt the bump and I was not a happy camper. I was more of a trembling traveller.

If we had gone over the side of the mountain, it was such rugged country, I believe that by the time we were discovered it is likely only our bones would be found. The problem was that I had this very terrifying thought, "We have to do this all over again in a few days on the way back." That was a thought I wished I had never thought.

Regardless of the terrifying ride we arrived safely at the town where we were to sleep and the next day we travelled by boat to the remote village. We set up our outreach on a basketball court (no matter how remote, every town has a basketball court). My job was to run the autoclave (sterilizer) and wash the dental equipment. The doctors were seeing patients at the other end of the court. I looked up and noticed an elderly man walking over to see the doctor. I got an impression in my mind immediately and the word was 'spiritual.'

I thought nothing more about it until the doctor called to me, "Hey, Warren this man has been deaf for five years; can you pray for him?"

Now it would have been incredibly unchristian of me to say "no" plus God had already told me what was wrong with him. I said, "Sure," and began to walk toward the man.

Just then I had this crazy thought. If it is a deaf spirit it might be hard of hearing. So I decided to yell into the man's ear, "DEAFNESS GET OUT, IN JESUS' NAME."

Instantly the man could hear in that ear. However, the other one was still deaf.

"Hmmm," I thought, "his 'brother' must be in this one," so I yelled in that ear, "DEAFNESS GET OUT, IN JESUS' NAME." Instantly he could hear in that ear too.

It's always good to see God miraculously heal someone in front of a doctor. The doctor who was also a believer checked him out as tears rolled down the man's face. Victory was achieved in his life. That is why it is so much fun hanging out with this God. You never know what He might do and it is not always easy to keep up with His program. I guess we just have to try the best we can, and it sometimes can be a scary ride as we step out in faith, in the natural and in the spiritual. As long as you are for Him, God is always there to catch you if you fall.

We managed to make it safely back down the mountain and I was less stressed believing in the driver to get us home safely after experiencing his very amazing driving skills on the way up. I guess it's a bit like our faith journey with God the more we experience Him in our life the more we trust Him.

DEAF MUTE

We were holding an outreach at a basketball court in Davao City Philippines our team of young people were with us. They had learnt some dramas which they performed to gather a crowd and after their performance we ministered to the people and prayed with those who wanted prayer.

Some teenage boys brought along a boy who was deaf and mute. He had never heard a sound in his life. He had no idea who I was and why his friends would want to bring him to this foreign person. I prayed for the Lord to heal him and what happened blew us all away. Instantly he could hear. His friends were so excited they began talking to him but he was in total bewilderment. There was noise going on all around him that he had never heard before. I will never forget the look of amazement on his face, he was almost as amazed as the rest of us. Because he had been deaf and mute all his life he had no idea what his friends were saying. We can't order miracles but we can expect them. Miracles are a supernatural act and remind us that our God is an awesome God.

The gift of healing is a blessing to be shared. Many who have a healing ministry can sometimes think there is a recipe to follow. Often, they tend to over emphasize the fact that Jesus was 100% human and play down the fact He was also 100% divine. He gave us the right of attorney to use His precious name to cast out demons and heal the sick. It is dangerous to think that we can be like God.

That idea tripped up Adam and Eve in the Garden of Eden and look at the mess that caused.

> *Now the serpent was more subtle* [crafty, cunning] *than any beast of the field which the Lord God had made. And he said unto the woman, Yea, hath God said, Ye shall not eat of every tree of the garden?*
>
> *And the woman said unto the serpent, We may eat of the fruit of the trees of the garden:*
>
> *But of the fruit of the tree which is in the midst of the garden, God hath said, Ye shall not eat of it, neither shall ye touch it, lest ye die.*
>
> *And the serpent said unto the woman, Ye shall not surely die:*
>
> *For God doth know that in the day ye eat thereof, then your eyes shall be opened, and ye shall be as gods, knowing good and evil.* (Genesis 3:1-5)

OH YE OF LITTLE FAITH

Once while trying to find work for my carpet cleaning business, I knocked on the front door of a house and got no answer. I decided to use the tradesman's entrance. Going around the back of the house I found an elderly couple sitting outside their back door. I introduced myself and said I was willing to give them a free demonstration of my machine and that way they would know if their carpet was due for a clean or not.

As I did my sales-pitch I noticed the man had a three-inch steel extension on the bottom of his right shoe. He definitely had one leg way shorter than the other. This got my attention and I had to ask him if I could pray for his leg to grow to be the same as the other. I said, "Before you answer, I must warn you: you will need to buy a new pair of shoes because you won't need the built up shoe anymore."

The man looked at me with a concerned look and after a while he said. "No, it's okay thanks."

Now I was a bit disappointed at his refusal. I wanted to see God do a number on this guy which would have been amazing but it wasn't to be.

I also noticed his wife had two hearing aids and was obviously quite deaf. I asked if I could pray for her hearing. She said she was willing. I asked her to remove her hearing aids. I asked the Lord to heal her and instantly she could hear in both ears.

Then the strangest thing happened. Standing there with her hearing aids in her hands she said, "What am I going to do with these?" and before I could answer, "give them to Jack Robinson", she stuck them back in her ears. I was stunned how both these people had such little faith. Her husband actually had more as he at least realized he would have had to buy a new pair of shoes.

Although I have witnessed many miracles, miracles don't always win souls for Christ. People need to hear the gospel as well, because the Bible says faith comes by hearing, and hearing by the Word of God. Being a nice neighbour doesn't get people saved either. Unless people understand the meaning of redemption and the need for it, they will remain lost.

Jesus healed a crippled man who was on a stretcher and lowered down through the roof, by his friends, to Jesus. He told the man his sins were forgiven (this upset the religious ones in the crowd) and then He healed him. The man stood up. Jesus told him to prove his healing by saying to him, "Take up thy bed and walk." He had to bend down to pick up his bed, something he couldn't do prior to meeting Jesus. Then he had to walk which he also couldn't do before he met Jesus. If only the lady had put her hearing aids anywhere else, but back in her ears, she might have had a testimony to tell of the healing power of Jesus.

So then faith cometh by hearing, and hearing by the word of God.
(Romans 10:17)

CURIOSITY KILLED THE HEADACHE

We held an outreach in Kawakawa and my wife was the preacher. After a few songs I was about to introduce Pauline to speak when I believed there were people with headaches in the audience, so I asked those with headaches to raise their hands.

A few people raised their hands and I prayed for them asking them to lower their hands as the pain left. All their hands dropped at the same time. That was pretty cool I thought. I later discovered, that when I asked those with headaches to put up their hands, a group of Mormon youth in attendance at the meeting decided to leave.

As they were going out one curious young Mormon who also had a headache went back to see what was happening and when he put his head through the door he was healed. When I heard about this I had a quiet chuckle, God is amazing. I don't know what happened to that young man. I do, however, know that God touched his life in a special way that he will always remember. Perhaps it may have caused him to seek the real Jesus of the Bible, instead of the Mormon Jesus who they claim is the brother of Satan.

TRANSVESTITE TRANSPORTATION TRIAL

I had been teaching at a Youth YWAM Discipleship Training School (DTS) in Manila and having some free time in the afternoon I decided to take a trip to the shopping mall in the next town.

I left the base and soon found a jeepney. A jeepney is a Filipino form of transport that originated after WWII from the abandoned US military jeeps. The Filipinos are very resourceful people and soon began using the jeeps as taxis. Then they figured out that if they lengthened them, they could carry more passengers. The stretched jeep is called a jeepney and they are a Filipino icon.

The jeepney was empty and I settled into the seat which ran length ways. I cannot sit up straight in a jeepney as they have a low ceiling which is okay for most Filipinos but not for anyone over 5'6".

I sat there waiting for the driver to start our short trip to town when all of a sudden I was joined by a group of men dressed as women. Makeup, earrings, wigs, high heels – the whole nine yards. Here I was sitting in the middle of ten transvestites. There was no way of being inconspicuous in this situation.

The vocal one of the group wanted to know what I was doing in the Philippines.

I quickly answered, "I'm a missionary."

I waited for the response, and I didn't have to wait long. "So, you hate homosexuals do you?"

Wow, this bloke, or should I say blokess, was going straight for the jugular. "No," I answered. "I am a Christian and a Christian is a follower of the teachings of Christ. Jesus has a problem with homosexuality, and if that's a problem for you, you need to take it up with Him. It's not for me to judge."

This seemed to take the wind out of his sails and halted his attack long enough for me to look compassionately at the one sitting on my right.

Looking at him I asked, "Wouldn't it be much easier for you to wake up in the morning and look in the mirror and say, 'Thank you God you made me a man' instead of having to pretend how you walk and talk all day long?"

The young man was quiet, as tears rolled down his cheeks. I must admit it was a weird moment in my life to be travelling to town surrounded by a bunch of guys dressed as girls. If you are willing to seize the moment, you never quite know where that will lead you.

> *And who is he that will harm you, if ye be followers of that which is good?*
>
> *But and if ye suffer for righteousness' sake, happy are ye: and be not afraid of their terror, neither be troubled;*
>
> *But sanctify the Lord God in your hearts: and be ready always to give an answer to every man that asks you a reason of the hope that is in you with meekness and fear...* (1 Peter 3:13-15)

| NEAR DEATH EXPERIENCE

In 2012 I was attending a medical outreach with a YWAM team from Kona who had joined our ministry in Mindoro Philippines. We travelled to the furthest town on our side of the island a place called Bulalacao. The church hosting the outreach provided accommodation for us in the church. We arrived on the Friday afternoon and after settling in, we attended their church service where I preached and played some music etc.

At the end of the preaching I asked if the person with the sore right elbow could come forward. A middle-aged man quickly came out from the congregation and I prayed asking the Lord to heal his elbow. He was suffering from tennis elbow (funny name for a health problem as there were no tennis courts in that town and I doubt many would know much about the game of tennis). He immediately received a healing. That was just the beginning of the most wonderful move of the healing power of God I have ever been privileged to witness. The church had been seriously praying for the outreach but especially praying for God's supernatural power to heal the sick.

The next morning before the outreach began I noticed hundreds of patients wanting to see a doctor. We only had one doctor, a wonderful man, in his 70s, with a heart for the poor, we also had a nurse who was training to be a doctor. We had two dentists and that was it for medical personnel. I said to the guys we need God to help us get the numbers down a bit. I was soon to preach before we started, which was something we always tried to do. However, this time I thought it needed something with some impact. I asked the guys to cover me with a sheet after I lay down on a bench stool, to make it look like I was dead. Carry me out and place me down in front of the people and look really sad.

This they did and as they lowered me down a hush came over the crowd. I didn't know what they might be thinking but it was a great atmosphere to preach about hell. As they were trying to figure out if I was dead or not, I jumped up with my Bible in my hand and with a panicked look I said, "I've been to hell, it's freaky, and you don't want to end up there."

I explained God's wonderful grace seen in the sacrifice of the Lord Jesus Christ who took our punishment on the cross, dying for our sins so we don't have to end up in hell. Many in the crowd received the Lord as their Saviour that morning. Praise God. I then asked all of the people with sore backs to line up over in the shade and I would pray for them. I ended up with about a dozen people. As I prayed for each one, they were healed instantly. I felt comfortable praying for sore backs as I had witnessed the Lord heal many over the years. However, that was not the end of it. News soon travelled to the rest of the people and soon I was confronted with all kinds of illnesses and problems. We had evangelists ready, to explain the good news of Jesus Christ to those waiting for prayer.

God showed up that day and healed every person who asked for prayer. People with high fevers and blood shot eyes were instantly healed. Deaf were healed and eyesight problems corrected. It was a wonderful thing to see. What a blessing for the church who had prayed for weeks for the outreach to be a success and for God to show up with signs and wonders. Regardless the greatest wonder of all is when a soul realizes they need a Saviour, to save them from themselves and a lost eternity, and then invite the Lord Jesus to come into their life.

Some people might have a problem with that style of preaching, thinking that we should not terrify people into believing in Christ. I don't do that kind of thing all the time but I believe it is biblical and the results that day saw God move in healing power in their hearts and bodies.

Keep yourselves in the love of God, looking for the mercy of our Lord Jesus Christ unto eternal life.
And of some have compassion, making a difference:
And others save with fear, pulling them out of the fire; hating even the garment spotted by the flesh. (Jude 1:21-23)

FAITH AS TINY AS A DOT

When I was training, the senior pastor suggested I have a healing meeting every Thursday afternoon. I loved doing that as I had to prepare a simple gospel message of around ten minutes in length, then I would pray for the sick.

I was quite excited for my first meeting and had made a sandwich sign and placed it by the footpath outside the church. That meeting was one of my largest gatherings; there must have been around twenty odd people turn up. I don't mean that they were odd people, just roughly twenty. Come to think of it, it was my largest meeting.

After I preached I invited those who wanted to be born again and those who needed physical healing to come forward. The lady first in line was a tiny woman called Dot. She wanted to give her life to Christ, and she did.

She said she also needed healing for her shoulder. She said she couldn't raise her right arm up because she was mauled by a cow many years prior.

I said to her, "It's awkward trying to raise both your arms to worship Jesus if one doesn't work. Let's see what the Lord wants to do." I placed my hand on her shoulder and prayed. To my surprise I felt her bone or something like a bone wriggling around under my hand. When I took my hand away she could lift her arm up. Thank you Jesus, I couldn't have had a better start to the weekly healing meetings.

That Sunday Dot came to see me and told me she had had a run in with her doctor. She said she told him that God had healed her shoulder.

The doctor was not as convinced as Dot was and said sarcastically, "You better get your lung done too then."

Dot said to me, with determination in her voice, "So I told him, I would."

I asked Dot what was wrong with her lung.

She told me that when the cow crushed her into the ground it broke her ribs and drove one through her lung and she only had one lung that worked. "Could you pray for my lung?"

I said, "Sure, let's see what God wants to do."

I prayed for Dot and God healed her lung, the next time I saw Dot she was so happy that she could walk around town and not have to keep stopping to take a rest and get her breath back.

Subsequent x-rays showed that her damaged lung was now working although it had shrunk over the years. Faith is what pleases the Lord. My pastor had enough faith to believe that (a) I had the gift of healing and (b) to ask me in to have a weekly healing meeting. I had enough faith to give it a go and Dot had faith to believe God could heal her. We had quite a few come to faith in Christ through those little healing meetings.

But without faith it is impossible to please him: for he that cometh to God must believe that he is, and that he is a rewarder of them that diligently seek him. (Hebrews 11:6)

WHEN 'GOD' CAME TO VISIT

While attending the Assemblies of God church during my early Christian life, our town or small city was a place where often those poor souls with mental problems were given their medication and set loose on the streets. Most of them were harmless but it was sad seeing them trapped in a mentally deranged space. One, quite a big guy, was under the delusion that he was God. It was common for him to attend a church and wait for the collection time. As the collection bag came past he would grab it and run for the door claiming that it was his money because he was 'God'.

This behaviour caused a bit of a stir in the Christian community and at the local police station, as police were often chasing 'god' around town to reclaim the offering bag.

One evening we were finishing off a series on evangelism at the church. I was on the piano playing a chorus to end the meeting when I noticed Ernie (not his real name) walk in as the leader closed in prayer and said the words, "And all the saints said, AMEN."

As I watched Ernie he said with authority, "I didn't say amen, because I am God!"

I decided to go and have a talk to 'god' and hopefully we could send him on his way back to the hospital, where he should have been, as it was possibly past his bedtime.

I talked with him, he was not keen to leave, and he pointed to

When 'god' Came to Visit

the name of the church on the wall beside him and said, "This is my church. Assemblies of God." Then he moved toward the leader, who had been taking the series. After some words were spoken he threw a punch at the leader.

"This guy is definitely not the real God," I thought. "I better do something about the situation." I moved around behind 'god' and jumped on him wrapping my arms around his neck from behind and hung on tight.

I knew that he was under the influence of demons or a demon and realized that not a lot of thought had gone into this act of bravery on my part. I was now in a very dangerous place. When someone is influenced by demonic spirits they have super strength. I knew what was going to happen so I braced myself for the fulfilment of my prophetic thought. I knew he would try to throw me over his head by bending down suddenly. I decided to hang on for dear life as I anticipated what was coming. My prophecy was right, he bent down suddenly trying to throw me off but I knew if I could hang on tight enough either his head would come off or we would both end up crashing to the floor. Fortunately, it was the latter.

We both went crashing to the deck. I jumped up just as three young men jumped on top of him to hold him down. He shook them off as if they were soft toys and leapt to his feet. His eyes were crazed and he was frothing at the mouth.

Just then in the midst of the most exciting meeting on evangelism I had ever attended I received a message from God (the real One). He just quietly said to me, "Warren," (He said my name, now that is cool), "we" (I assumed he meant me when He said we, because he doesn't fight Satan, doesn't have to, the battle is already won at that end) "we don't fight against flesh and blood."

That text is straight out of the Bible so I pointed at Ernie and commanded the religious demon to leave. In a moment, as if God

Seizing the Moment

switched the light on, Ernie shook his head and snapped out of his deranged state. He looked around in bewilderment and walked over to the corner as quiet as a lamb and sat down.

When the ruckus first started my wife went and rang for the police and the timing was perfect. As soon as Ernie sat down two policemen walked in and quietly escorted him back to the hospital.

Satan does not play fair; Jesus said he is the destroyer, the father of lies, the old dragon that deceives the world. Jesus on the other hand is the way the truth and the life. I learned that night that you can take God at His word; He will never let you down. Even when our human instincts kick in and we make mistakes He is there to get you back on course.

Like I said, Satan doesn't play fair and is out to destroy whoever he can. One day while walking the streets of town, Ernie met another guy from the mental ward walking toward him. He stopped for a conversation and during the conversation Ernie told the guy that he was Jesus. The other guy informed him that he was mistaken and that he was really Judas and that he (the other guy) was Jesus. Ernie was shocked and asked him if he was sure. The guy was very sure. Not long after that they found Ernie hanging from a tree; sadly he had believed a lie and taken his life in the same manner as Judas.

MY SON THE SUNDAY SCHOOL APOLOGIST

My son Brad was a little man of faith, and brought a lot of joy to his mum and me. His Sunday School teacher was telling the little kids about Moses over the course of a few weeks. When she got to the last lesson, she told the children that Moses never entered the Promised Land.

Well this statement must have fired up Brad's apologetic (full on Bible study) juices. He put up his hand and said that was not right, Moses did enter the Promised Land.

The Sunday school teacher reassured Brad that the Bible says that Moses did not enter the Promised Land.

Brad then said, "My dad says he did."

By this time the teacher was beginning to get a bit agitated. "I don't care what your father says; Moses never went into the Promised Land."

After the service Brad came up to me and said, "Dad, where's the scripture that says Moses went into the Promised Land? My Sunday school teacher says he didn't."

I told him it was in Matthew 17:1-3. Then I said to Brad. "He just popped in a bit later for a short visit." Brad ran off to tell the Sunday school teacher.

And after six days Jesus takes Peter, James, and John his brother, and brings them up into an high mountain apart,

> *And was transfigured before them: and his face did shine as the sun, and his raiment was white as the light.*
> *And, behold, there appeared unto them Moses and Elijah talking with him.*

Brad was the youngest (of seven children) and was like a sponge as he listened to our family conversations. We attended teacher parent day to see how he was going in his second year of primary school. The teacher told us that she was very impressed by his vocabulary and said she had asked the class a question. The question went something like this. What if I thought something was true but it wasn't? Brad's hand shot up and said, "You would be having a cognitive distortion." Unbeknown to the teacher, that had been the family fun phrase for the previous week.

WITNESSING AT A NUDIST BEACH

Pauline and I decided to take Brad to the beach for the day so he could swim and play in the sand. We arrived at our destination which was not far from our home. I had been there years before when I was young, a lovely sandy beach with not many people, the perfect spot to relax and have some time out.

There was nobody in sight as we arrived and laid out our beach towels on the sand. Brad was keen to rearrange the beach and headed off with his bucket and spade. As we lay in the sun enjoying the peace and tranquillity and the sound of the waves crashing on the shore, I heard some people arrive and heard them talking to a child. We took no notice and occasionally would look through one eye down the beach to see Brad was okay. After a while I looked and saw him playing in the sand with a little girl, chatting away and having fun.

Not long after we heard the little girl call out to her Mum, "Hey Mum, I'm a Christian now."

"That's nice," said the Mum.

When Pauline and I looked up, to see who it was Brad had been talking with, we discovered the mum and dad were both stark naked.

In my absence the area had become a nudist beach. We thought to be there clothed was not fair to the nudists so it was either join them or leave. We chose the latter and laughed all the way home totally proud of our little sandcastle evangelist.

SHOCKING THE SPECIALIST

I was staying at a friend's place in Tauranga NZ and was about to leave when his wife asked me to pray for her. She was having an ear operation that morning and was feeling a bit anxious. She had been checked by her ear specialist and had a hole in her eardrum. The doctor was going to take a skin graft and place it over the hole. Now I thought that was pretty clever that people can do such wonderful things these days with surgical knowledge and skill.

As I prayed, I asked God to calm her nerves and guide the doctor's hands and that the operation would go really well etc. I then said goodbye and left for Auckland.

The following day I realized I had lost my diary and gave my friend a call to see if I had left it at his house. His wife answered the phone and said they hadn't found it but she had something to tell me about her operation. She said the doctor numbed her ear and took the skin graft then went to place it over the hole but the hole was no longer there.

She said the doctor was shocked and bewildered, saying, "This has never happened to me before in all my practice." She told him that she had prayer before she came and he replied, "You should have told me before I numbed your ear." On testing he discovered her hearing had improved by 30% in that ear.

I was pretty chuffed at hearing her story. God is wonderful, caring and exciting and will never cause you to have a boring existence if you want to walk with him through this crazy old world.

Crazy? The Bible says before Jesus returns things will be crazy. White will be black, black will be white. Good will be evil and evil, good. 'He's' will want to be 'she's' and 'she's' will want to be 'he's'. The 'selfie' generation is upon us.

> *Woe unto them that call evil good, and good evil; that put darkness for light, and light for darkness; that put bitter for sweet, and sweet for bitter!* (Isaiah 5:20)

GENEROSITY MISSED THE POINT (MATERIALISTIC MISHAP)

When we sold our dairy farm we purchased a small block of land closer to town and found ourselves just down the road from an old school friend who I hadn't seen since my rugby days. I had a little 35 horsepower tractor with a frontend loader. It was a great little tractor and my friend thought so too. He would borrow it now and again to get work done on his small block. Being newly saved and full of zeal I used to try and witness to my friend. This is often not an easy thing to do. I was able to convince him to come to a church meeting where we had a travelling evangelist who had the gift of healing. I wanted him to see the power of God happening before his eyes. I thought this will get him into the kingdom of God.

He had said to me, "I won't believe it unless I see it."

I was pleased he had laid down a challenge and agreed to come to church. It was an evening service and after the evangelist had spoken, he called for those with sore backs and a few came forward. Now my trap was set. I had my friend come up the front with me to watch the miracle take place. My friend was not of tall stature and as the person's leg was about to grow out to the same length as the other some big guy came and stood right in front of my friend and it was all over and he missed "seeing" the miracle for himself.

I was not about to give up so I went to visit him a few days later with a different approach. I knew how much he liked my tractor so I said he could have it. I said, "One day the Lord is coming back for His Church and all the Christians are going to disappear. If this were to happen, I want you to go and help yourself to my tractor." Then I added, "I would really rather you came with me." Thinking that this would have a spiritual effect on his life I was interested in his response.

He thought for a while as I waited in anticipation for some spiritual breakthrough. My thoughts were interrupted by his very sincere response. He said, as he leaned on the strainer post and gazed over his little patch of land, "Warren, you are the first person to leave me anything."

I guess he was touched and I had caused my friend to be aware of the rapture and to look forward to it. However, I think he saw it from a different perspective, the rapture would mean that he would get my tractor and get rid of his crazy Christian neighbour.

IN THE POO MORE WAYS THAN ONE

Another neighbour needed some help on his horticulture property. He told me he would pay me if I could come and give him a hand. He had planted a few hundred peppers and needed to have fertilizer spread around them. He was very pleased that he had secured free fertilizer. The product was a couple of truckloads of waste from the town council's sewerage plant. I didn't share his enthusiasm but agreed to get started.

My neighbour was a character and had a bit of a resemblance to Groucho Marks. He had called into our place a few weeks prior to ask if I would go and talk with his wife about God stuff. She had been getting visits from the Jehovah's Witnesses, and he was worried. I said I would and went to see his wife one afternoon to see if I could set her straight. It was around afternoon smoko (afternoon break) when I went there and placed my bible on the table. I was as keen as pig in a bucket of yogurt. Just as I was getting started the workers came crashing in on my Bible study.

I was not prepared for such an intrusion and before they had even placed themselves in a chair around the table, they began asking questions. I was now surrounded with Kiwi guys who would rather use me for a bashing ball so the lesson tended to draw to an end. I told his wife I would come back that evening and bring Pauline with me.

As we arrived that evening her husband said a quick hi and shot out the door. After sharing the gospel message with her I said, "Well we better be going."

Pauline gave me a bit of a dig and said, "Aren't you going to pray with her to become a Christian?"

I whispered, "I don't know how it goes."

I looked at our friend and she was quite convicted, hoping her heart kept beating until these two 'Christians' figured out how to ease her anxiety.

We bumbled our way through a prayer which she repeated and I looked at Pauline and she looked at me, and we realized we had led our first soul to Christ. What a buzz. A few weeks later she got baptized.

Now back to the peppers and cheap fertilizer. As I worked with this amazingly cheap fertilizer placing it around the plants, I told my friend about what the Bible said was going to happen in the end times.

Now he did very well I guess, after about four hours of me going on and on he finally snapped, "That's it! I'm sick of you @&%* Christians, you're always judging."

I replied, "No I'm not, I'm just telling you what the Bible says."

That was definitely 'it' I had pushed him over the edge. "Get out," he shouted, so I got up and left. He was as mad as a foxy in a room full of rats and as I walked home he went inside and rang Pauline, and told her that I was not to come back to his place rah-di-rah.

I had really upset him that was for sure. I was obviously not good at this friendship evangelism and I never heard from him or saw him for about two weeks.

As I was working on my tractor one morning, he came walking sheepishly along my driveway towards me. "Hi," I said, making out all was well.

As he approached, he said, "I was pretty angry with you the

other day. I was so angry at what you said that I jumped in my car and drove to town to buy a Bible." He told me he had been reading it right through and when he was near the end a scripture kind of jumped out at him. It said, "…you should get baptized." He informed me that he had been angry about his wife getting baptized and said, "I am willing to be baptized."

Now you usually get baptized after you become a Christian not before, but who was I to argue. I said, "That's great, I will book you in."

I thought to myself, "If God is on his case he will surely be saved by Sunday." I went inside and called my pastor.

My pastor assumed my neighbour was a Christian and said, "Okay that's great."

He was saved that week and baptized Sunday. The Bible talks about seed (God's Word) landing on fertile ground; perhaps there was more fertilizer around that day than I realized and some landed in the heart of my neighbour. Praise God. Could this be classed as a form of 'friendship evangelism?' Get them so mad they go and buy a Bible? I decided most probably not.

| UNWANTED RESURRECTION

I was speaking at a home-group in Tauranga one night. The home belonged to an elderly widow in her 80s. I mentioned the rapture and said, "One day Jesus is coming for His church (followers) and is going to change our bodies from mortal to immortal in a fraction of a second. Then He is going to call us up to meet Him in the clouds." I explained that the souls that are in heaven have not yet received their resurrection bodies and will receive them at the time of the rapture. I read the following verses:

> *Behold, I show you a mystery; We shall not all sleep, but we shall all be changed,*
> *In a moment, in the twinkling of an eye, at the last trump: for the trumpet shall sound, and the dead shall be raised incorruptible, and we shall be changed.* (1 Corinthians 15:51-52)

> *But I would not have you to be ignorant, brethren, concerning them which are asleep [dead believers], that ye sorrow not, even as others which have no hope.*
> *For if we believe that Jesus died and rose again, even so them also which sleep in Jesus will God bring with him* [he will bring the spirits of the believers who have died back with Him when He comes for His church].
> *For this we say unto you by the word of the Lord, that we which*

are alive and remain unto the coming of the Lord shall not prevent [precede] *them which are asleep.*

For the Lord himself shall descend from heaven with a shout, with the voice of the archangel, and with the trump of God: and the dead in Christ shall rise [stand up on the earth] *first:*

Then we which are alive and remain [living believers] *shall be caught up together with them in the clouds, to meet the Lord in the air: and so shall we ever be with the Lord.*

Wherefore comfort one another with these words. (1 Thessalonians 4:13-18)

The lady looked at me in shock, and began whispering to the young woman on her right. I asked her what was wrong and she said, "I don't want my husband getting a new body and popping up in the front garden." That was where she had sprinkled his ashes. She said she sprinkled the other half in the harbour.

"Perhaps you will have to have two husbands," I said.

This really did put fear into her mind. I then had to explain that it will be okay, she won't have two husbands, and in fact she won't have any.

For in the resurrection they neither marry, nor are given in marriage, but are as the angels of God in heaven. (Matthew 22:30)

She calmed down after I explained that to her. After the meeting I prayed for the sick and I remember she wanted prayer for her sore back. I had her sit in a chair and checked her legs to see if they were the same. One was longer so I asked if she wanted to be shorter or taller.

She said, "Taller."

I have never found a woman who said she wanted to be shorter.

God brought her legs to be the same length and took all the pain out of her back.

Two years later I was praying for the sick at a Baptist church and I noticed an elderly lady waiting over to my right. I finished praying and she came over to me.

I asked what would she like me to pray for, she said, "Oh no, I don't want prayer. You came to my house and led a home-group. You prayed for my back and I just wanted to encourage you. My back has been fine ever since and I am able to get out and work in the garden." She never mentioned anything about her husband or her objection to him resurrecting in her garden. I'm guessing he was well and truly laid to rest.

ABSCESSED TOOTH

I was helping to pack up the sound gear after an outreach in a suburb of Whangarei NZ when one of our team asked me if I would go outside and pray for a girl with a sore tooth. When I saw her, I realized she was in a lot of pain. Her jaw was swollen and when I touched it, it was hot. Thinking that she was a Christian and one of the youth group from the church we were working with, I asked her if she believed Jesus could heal her.

She shrugged her shoulders and looked at me with a strange look (like, what planet do you come from?).

I said, "He can, and He will."

I put my hand on her cheek and prayed for the Lord to heal her. God healed her instantly and she responded with a startled look as she felt her face wondering where the pain and swelling had gone.

The sad thing was that she didn't want to commit her life to the Lord. The next night at church a young man came to see me. He told me that he was watching from the shadows and saw what God did to the girl with the abscessed tooth. He told me he knew her and that she couldn't care less about Jesus but he watched as Jesus healed her anyway. He thought to himself, "That's the God I want to follow." The young man gave his life to the Lord that night.

One of the things that makes Christianity such an amazing faith is seeing what God does when faith is released into a situation. We might be expecting God to do something in the way we think He will do it. He does things in the way He wants to and it can be very unexpected.

For my thoughts are not your thoughts, neither are your ways my ways, saith the Lord. (Isaiah 55:8)

ANOTHER TOOTH STORY

I was asked to play some background music for a garden party fundraiser for my wife's orphanage in the Philippines. While having lunch I sat with an old school friend who I had caught up with again after fifty years.

It is hard to make old friends when you are old, so best make them when you are young. She had brought her friend from England with her but sadly she was suffering from a gum infection that was causing her terrific pain. My friend rushed off to her car to get a pill for her pain. When she returned I told them the previous story about the girl with the abscessed tooth.

She looked at me and said, "Can you pray for me?"

I reached out and placed my hand on her cheek and prayed that Jesus would heal her. I took my hand away and sat down.

Then we noticed a look of disbelief come over her as she said, "It's gone."

We were all touched by the goodness of God so much so that the lady began to pray quietly to God with lovely gratitude for what He had just done. I love watching the reaction of people when God blesses them with instant healings.

| UNSTEADY SAILOR

I picked up a good job cleaning the carpets in cabins on New Zealand's coastal oil tankers. One day I needed to go and buy more dust bags for my cleaner. One of the sailors heard I was going to town and, having been stuck on the ship for months, he was quite keen to come for a ride.

We piled into my old Nissan C20 van and headed for town. Lots of talk on the way about nothing until I arrived at the shop where I picked up some vacuum bags. On the way back I noticed my newfound sailor friend was very nervous being back on land again. He had become unfamiliar with the motion of travelling on the highway. To add to his uneasiness, in a van you are sitting right up the front with nothing like a big engine that might save you from an oncoming vehicle or trees that could jump out in front of you.

Observing this I thought to myself, "The Bible says 'the fear of the Lord is the beginning of wisdom.'" I reached for my Bible which was beside me on the engine cover between the two front seats. I began to tell him about the cashless system and the tattoo or mark of the beast. The New World Order and the coming Antichrist. I said, "I will show you in the Bible," and started thumbing the pages to find the spot.

While I was fumbling through the pages I deliberately veered the van over to the edge of the road until it began to bump along the edge of the tar seal. Also in a van the front seats are directly over the front wheels. Now I really had his attention and he quickly offered to find the place I was looking for in the Bible.

I thought, "Now this is going well. He has the fear of the Lord in amongst the fear of the driver, is holding the Bible and desperately trying to find a scripture that he has no idea of its whereabouts, and when he finds it he is going to read it out loud."

With some guidance he managed to find it and read it out to me. It is amazing how things can happen so *quickly*. That little Bible study should be lodged in his brain and hopefully we meet again in heaven.

So then faith cometh by hearing, and hearing by the word of God.
(Romans 10:17)

Blessed is he that reads, and they that hear the words of this prophecy, and keep those things which are written therein: for the time is at hand. (Revelation 1:3)

| BUSY DAY

One day I had to travel to a small town about 20 miles from home. My first job was for a man who was recovering from heart bypass surgery. I began my cleaning and after a while he offered me a coffee.

As I sat and chatted with him, I asked him, "If you were to die, do you know if you will go to heaven?" I assumed he had been thinking a lot about that after having such a major operation.

He said he didn't know.

I felt that he was a person who needed to have salvation explained by using a diagram. I got a piece of paper and began to explain what happens when you receive salvation. I drew a small circle and filled it in leaving the shape of a key hole. Then I wrote "spirit". I drew another circle around that one and wrote "soul". Then I wrote "emotions and memories". I then drew another circle around that one and wrote "body", and the five senses. I then explained the meaning of what Jesus meant when He said we must be born again if we want to enter heaven.

Jesus answered and said unto him, Verily, verily, I say unto thee, Except a man be born again, he cannot see the kingdom of God.

Nicodemus saith unto him, How can a man be born when he is old? can he enter the second time into his mother's womb, and be born?

Jesus answered, Verily, verily, I say unto thee, Except a man be

> *born of water and of the Spirit, he cannot enter into the kingdom of God.* (John 3:3-5)

I explained, before we receive salvation we are separated from God because of sin, and our spirit is dead. However, God has made our spirit with a vacancy in it that only one person can fill. That person is Jesus. The Bible says that when we were dead in our trespass and sin Christ died for us. When we ask Jesus to come into our life, He does just that. He comes and fills the empty void in our spirit with his spirit and resurrects it to life. This causes a chain reaction in our person. Our spirit begins to have contact with God and with our soul and our soul then influences our body. This is the opposite of how we react when our life is controlled by the desires of our mind and body. It is so simple but incredibly amazing because from that time on, once you have allowed Jesus to be part of your life, He will guide you and teach you how to live for Him. Jesus gives you the ability to turn from your sin and experience the freedom in your spirit that is now being born again.

> *That which is born of the flesh is flesh; and that which is born of the Spirit is spirit.*
> *Marvel not that I said unto thee, Ye must be born again.*
> *The wind blows where it lists, and thou hears the sound thereof, but can not tell where it comes, and where it goes: so is every one that is born of the Spirit.* (John 3:6-8)

He was willing to pray with me and accept Jesus as his Saviour. After finishing his carpet, I left for the local town to do some door knocking and soon I found myself talking to a young couple with a three-month old baby. The baby was struggling to breathe due to Asthma. The baby's tiny lungs were full of fluid. I asked if I could pray for the baby and they agreed. Placing my hand on the tiny chest I prayed and the Lord instantly healed the baby. There was no sign of fluid being coughed up, and breathing just instantly became normal. It was a wonderful miracle to see.

Next I had an appointment at another house and went to start that carpet. I met the lady of the house, her husband was at work. It turned out that we knew each other as we both lived in the same town prior our shifting. I cleaned her carpet and during a cup of tea I was able to share the good news with her. She had been raised in a church that practiced a lot of man-made traditions and religious rites that were contradictory to the Bible's teachings. She was very receptive and we prayed and she accepted the Lord Jesus as her Saviour. I had heard that there was a Presbyterian minister in the town that believed in baptism by full immersion. I knew that although I had never met him, he must be putting the Bible first for true teaching so I told her to attend his church.

A LITTLE TASTE OF HEAVEN

Two years later after I had been preaching in a nearby town a chap came and asked me if I was still doing carpet cleaning.

I said, "Now and again."

He said, "Don't give that up."

I asked him why.

He asked me if I remembered Mrs Brown (not her real name).

I was not sure who he was talking about.

He said, "You led her to Jesus and told her to go to the Presbyterian Church."

I remembered then who he meant.

He told me she joined the church I had suggested to her and she is now leading the prayer team. He also told me about the guy with the heart bypass and how he had given his life to the Lord. He said that the man's sister had told him about it and that it was an answer to prayer as she had been praying for her brother for years.

I believe that is what is going to happen in heaven if we are willing to share our faith with others. Heaven is all about testimonies.

I have planted, Apollos watered; but God gave the increase.

So then neither is he that plants anything, neither he that waters; but God that gives the increase.

Now he that plants and he that waters are one: and every man shall receive his own reward according to his own labour. (1 Corinthians 3:8-7)

NEVER GIVE UP

My carpet cleaning job took me to an elderly couple's house, an hour from home, at a lovely beach. As I cleaned, the man, in his mid-eighties, followed me around watching my every move. I tried to lure him into conversation but he didn't seem interested in any subject I brought up. I tried politics, fishing, sport, rocking chairs but there was no response.

By lunchtime he had figured out I was a Christian and as we sat at the table he began to speak. He said, "We believe that you should try and get along with your neighbours, pay your bills and love your kids etc."

I said, "That's all very good but it won't get you into heaven." I sensed a negative reaction to my words as the meal table chatter ceased to an awkward silence. I realized also at that moment I hadn't finished the job or been paid. I excused myself from the table and went back to my cleaning. I prayed to God to give me a breakthrough as I was about finished the job.

I asked the couple if either of them suffered from a bad back. This idea hadn't come from, what is known in Christian ministry as a word of knowledge, it was an estimated guess.

The wife in her late seventies answered, "Yes, he has."

We were in the lounge so I suggested he lie down on the floor and I would see if his pelvis is out of line. He lay down with his feet pointing to his wife's TV chair and I noticed quite a difference in the length of his legs.

I asked his wife to sit in her chair and I sat in his chair as he lay on his back stretched out on the floor. I then looked at her and said, "You watch this, it is better than watching the soaps on TV. God is going to make his legs the same length." I asked the Lord to heal his back and make his legs the same length, and sure enough his leg grew out and he started making kind of pleasant moaning sounds. The Holy Spirit had come upon him and he was experiencing a wonderful sensation of healing. I helped him to his feet and asked if there was anything else he needed healed.

His wife answered (strange how wives often answer on behalf, before the husband can get a word out), "He can't raise his right arm."

Jokingly I said, "How can you praise God like that?" I prayed for his arm to be healed and next thing he is lifting it up fully stretching, walking around the lounge swinging his arm up and down.

Now things were going well and his wife had a surge of faith. She said, "I have a crook knee."

"What's wrong with your knee?"

"Arthritis," she said. She lifted her right leg off the floor and swung it like a pendulum and I could hear a horrible grating sound.

I prayed for the pain in her leg to go and immediately it left. However, the grating sound was still there. I looked at her and said, "I think you need the Lord to give you a lube job." I prayed to the Lord to give her a lube job while I swung her leg back and forth. The grating suddenly stopped, and she was so excited.

She then said, "You must be an angel sent from God."

I said that I wasn't, just a Bible-believing Christian. I thought this could be my only chance to seize the moment, so I suggested we hold hands and give thanks to God in a prayer.

I asked them to follow me in the prayer. As I prayed, I added the sinner's prayer and we asked Jesus into our hearts. I hope and pray they were born again after the demonstration of God's love and grace through His healing power.

> *For by grace are ye saved through faith; and that not of yourselves: it is the gift of God:*
> *Not of works, lest any man should boast.* (Ephesians 2:8-9)

NOSE BLEEDER

I was approached by a man who just lived a kilometre down the road on a small farm. He wanted to know if I would come and pray for his son who suffered from nose bleeds. He and his wife were not believers but someone must have mentioned me to them. I said I would and arranged a time to see their son. When I arrived I met the boy, a teenager, and as I was about to minister to him the parents quickly left the room. They had sensed it was something spiritual that was affecting the boy. I talked with the lad and told him that I would pray for his bleeding problem and that Jesus could heal him. I prayed for him and left.

Months later the man was passing by and he said, "I don't know what was going on in the room when you were praying but it sure sounded like you were wrestling with something." I thought to myself that I must have burst out in tongues or something unfamiliar to him and he thought I was in some kind of spiritual fight. He said that his son had not had another nose bleed since that day. I do know that Christians have amazing angelic creatures looking out for us and that Jesus is their mighty captain. Perhaps they showed up that day while I prayed.

> *But to which of the angels said he at any time, Sit on my right hand, until I make thine enemies thy footstool?*
>
> *Are they not all ministering spirits, sent forth to minister for them who shall be heirs of salvation?* (Hebrews 1:13-14)

CALLING FOR BACKUP

One evening we were showing a video to our youth group in our lounge when I decided it was time for a coffee break.

As everyone was leaving the lounge and heading for the dining room one of the youth came over to me looking a bit strange. He said, "Can I have some prayer? I'm not feeling good, I think I need deliverance."

I quickly grabbed the two strongest guys in the group and got them to sit either side of him to hold him down as I prayed. He sure did have some tormenting spirits messing with him. He took some restraining but after a few prayers we had managed to cast them all out except one.

Now this one was very smart and was doing its best to get me mad. They do this to get the one praying to forget that the fight is taking place in the spirit realm and in that realm their fight is over if the Christian knows their authority in Christ.

He looked at me and laughed, and said in a growly mocking voice, "You can't get rid of me, I've been here for ages."

I thought that this demon was definitely not much of a mathematician as the young man was only eighteen years old.

After some more prayer we seemed to be getting nowhere and I was getting sick of this thing laughing at me I must admit. I looked at him and said, "I am going to ask the Father to send some angels to deal with you." The demon then laughed as I bowed my head and closed my eyes to pray. I managed to get one word out which was 'Father' and he let out a horrific scream of absolute terror.

I looked and his eyes were sticking out like golf balls. The scream came up from inside him out through his mouth and out through the roof and was gone.

He looked at me and said, "Did you see that?"

I said, "See what?"

He then said, "Two angels came walking out through the wall, their heads were as high as the ceiling (our ceiling was 11'6") and they walked straight at the thing in me, the thing in me became terrified and took off."

He was set free and went on to be a very strong Christian. Jesus is the captain of the angelic hosts of heaven and there are a lot of them.

A police training class was once asked, "What would you do if you had to arrest your mother for a crime?"

One young recruit quickly replied, "Call for backup."

It is good that Christians can also call for backup.

RAPTURE READY

Perhaps I need to explain this future event spoken of in the Bible before I tell this next story. The word rapture is from a Latin word meaning to snatch away or to be caught up, to depart or departure. Jesus promised His believers that in the last days He would come and rescue them from the coming horrific judgements that are going to come upon the earth. Referred to in the Bible as the wrath of God. Jesus taught this new teaching at the Last Supper:

> *Let not your heart be troubled: ye believe in God, believe also in me.*
>
> *In my Father's house are many mansions: if it were not so, I would have told you. I go to prepare a place for you.*
>
> *And if I go and prepare a place for you, I will come again, and receive you unto myself; that where I am, there ye may be also.* (John 14:1-3)

Jesus mentions it again in Revelation:

> *Because thou hast kept the word of my patience, I also will keep thee from the hour of temptation, which shall come upon all the world, to try them that dwell upon the earth.* (Revelation 3:10)

When this wonderful event takes place the believers' bodies will be changed in the fraction of a second and they will be caught up (raptured) to meet the Lord Jesus in the clouds and be taken to the Father's house in heaven.

> *For the Lord himself shall descend from heaven with a shout, with the voice of the archangel, and with the trump of God: and the dead in Christ shall rise first:*
> *Then we which are alive and remain shall be caught up together with them in the clouds, to meet the Lord in the air: and so shall we ever be with the Lord.*
> *Wherefore comfort one another with these words.* (1 Thessalonians 4:16-18)

I have always loved this promise in the word of God. One day I was flying out of Nelson New Zealand and sitting beside me was a young guy about nineteen years old. I had a window seat and was enjoying the buzz I get when flying as the plane rises up into the sky (I have a fear of heights).

After a while when we had almost reached the top of the climb, I turned to the young guy and said, "Man! One day I am going to do this without an aeroplane under me."

He looked at me rather strangely so I asked him if he had ever heard of the rapture. He said he hadn't. I said, "Don't worry, heaps of Christians haven't either." I told him all about this amazing event that is going to happen at any moment because no one knows when it will be. He seemed to be quite interested.

When we landed we got off the plane and I could see him a few passengers in front of me. He had to catch another plane and headed off in the other direction for his next flight. He walked a few paces and must have caught me out the corner of his eye. Instead of ducking his head and running, he spun round and came running over to me.

Seizing the Moment

He put out his hand and shook mine and said, "Thanks for telling me that stuff man, that's awesome." Then off he went.

> *Watch ye therefore, and pray always, that ye may be accounted worthy to escape all these things that shall come to pass, and to stand before the Son of man.* (Luke 21:36)

Are you rapture ready?

POWER OF THE MEMORIZED SCRIPTURES

I was flying from Sydney back to Auckland and sitting beside me was a big strong guy looking a bit battered around. I asked him what he had been up to. He said he was in an Auckland team that played American football and was coming back from some games in Sydney. We got talking about all sorts of things. Whenever he said something that I could agree with, I would just slip a scripture into the mix. I would say, "You know you're right; the Bible says…" then I would quote a scripture. This happened about seven or eight times. I did it very naturally as we talked.

Then I noticed his countenance changed and he began to stare into space. I thought to myself, "Holy Spirit is here."

He remained staring at the one spot on the ceiling somewhere for what seemed ages. Then he looked at me and said, "I'm glad I got seat number 35E. Thanks for talking with me."

I said, "While we were talking I was slipping the word of God into our conversation and because your spirit is open, God is able to minister to your spirit." I think this might have spooked him a wee bit and so I added, "Someone is praying for you."

Now this really got his attention. "How do you know that?"

I said, "Your spirit is open to the word of God and that often is the case if someone is praying for you."

"Fair go?" Then he looked at me and said, "I know who it is too. It's my uncle and aunty."

I asked him if he wanted to give his life to Jesus.

He said, "No, not right now."

I told him to go and see his uncle and aunty as soon as he could, as they would know what's best for him.

Time flies when you're having fun and we were soon on the ground at Auckland.

For the word of God is quick, and powerful, and sharper than any two edged sword, piercing even to the dividing asunder of soul and spirit, and of the joints and marrow, and is a discerner of the thoughts and intents of the heart. (Hebrews 4:12)

TEACHING MY STUDENTS TO SEIZE THE MOMENT

Pauline and I ran a small Bible School as part of church activities. We had nine students and taught on many topics. When the Church had guest speakers, we would ask them to come and speak to the students.

One week I taught on evangelism and after three days of lectures decided to take the students to the local town. I picked the busiest day of the week which was Thursday; the day the unemployment benefit was paid. The mall was full of likely candidates to hear the good news about Jesus. I told them to mingle and ask God to show them who He wanted them to speak to. I found a guy with a broken arm and sat down beside him and introduced myself and chatted for a while but he was not receptive so I said good bye and moved on.

I found a group of young street kids and asked them who in their group was the brainiest. They all pointed at the same boy. I pulled out a card and asked him to read what it said. There was a trick to the wording on the front which had three triangles. In each triangle was a phrase. 'A bird in the hand', 'Paris in the Spring' and another which I can't remember. Each one actually read 'A bird in *the the* hand' and 'Paris in *the the* spring'. I then asked him to turn it over and read what it said on the back.

He was full of confidence and began to read, "You read a bird in the hand but it said the the hand. As you assumed it just said one 'the' you probably also assume God will send you to hell. No, He doesn't, you send yourself. Because God so loved the world that He gave His only Begotten Son that all who believe in Him will not perish but receive everlasting life (John 3:16)."

I said to the boys, "He just preached the gospel. Do you know what can happen when someone preaches the gospel?"

They looked curiously at me.

I then said, "The Bible says that signs and wonders will follow. Which one of you has a sore back?"

The smallest boy said, "I have."

I got him to put his legs out straight and there was definitely a difference in length. I also noticed this street kid was wearing new Doc Martin boots, I didn't ask where they came from. I then asked God to heal him and make his legs the same length and He did. The boy knew straight away he was healed and the group became very excited.

The questions began to fly and one said, "What about the Mormons?"

I said, "Never mind about the Mormons, what about you?"

One boy then asked me, "Can you do arms?"

I said, "I can't do arms but God can, why do you ask?"

One of his arms was shorter than the other. He held his hands out with palms together and sure enough there was quite a difference. I prayed and his arm grew out. Now this caused the young guy to jump around in circles in total amazement.

I was having such a good time with these boys I thought it about time to check on my students. I looked to see where they were, thinking they would all spread out among the people. I was shocked to see they had gathered in a group off to the side and had been watching me the whole time.

Then one of the students shook his head and said to the others, "Come on guys back to class."

So, we went back to class for a debriefing session.

DANGERS WHEN ONE KISSES A TREE TOO HARD

After preaching in a lovely South Island town called Wanaka we were invited to a pot luck lunch. As I glanced over the people there, I noticed a young man who caught my attention. His speech was a bit different but I had no idea what the reason was. Pauline and I filled our plates with lovely home cooked food prepared with good old South Island hospitality and sat down.

The young man I mentioned came and sat down beside me. He was very talkative and was soon sharing his testimony with me. He had suffered a horrific car crash in which the car went sideways at great speed into a tree. He was in the back seat and took the full impact. His face was crushed in on the left side and he was in a coma for a month. His face had been reconstructed with surgical steel and he had lost his hearing in his left ear and also his taste and smelling senses were gone. He was a very positive young man so I asked, and he agreed, that I could pray for his hearing to be restored.

God healed his hearing so well that he seemed to have super hearing. Perhaps it had something to do with the titanium in his face by his ear. I was quietly talking to Pauline with my back to him and he was repeating what I was saying. I was amazed how well he could hear.

He told me he had lost his taste and smelling senses. He asked, "Do you think God might make them too strong?" He was afraid that if his smelling was as acute as his hearing there might be smells he would rather not know about.

I assured him that God knows what is best for us and that he had no need to worry.

After he gave me the go ahead to pray he told me that he would test his smelling on the ham he had on his plate. Ham does not give off a strong smell so I agreed that would be a good test. I prayed for him and he slowly lifted his plate up to his nose and 'bingo' he could smell the ham.

The God of the Bible is a supernatural God. Trying to work out methods or remedies for operating in the gift of healing is something I don't do but all the best to those who think they have figured it out. I believe healing is a gift from God to be used to bless others and if one believes as a child taking God at His word that's enough. The reason they are called miracles is because we don't know how He does them. New Age gurus will tell you it's karma, vibrations, positive thinking or being one with the universe etc. My God is an awesome God and nothing comes close to what he can do for those who love Him.

> *But as it is written, Eye hath not seen, nor ear heard, neither have entered into the heart of man, the things which God hath prepared for them that love him.* (1 Corinthians 2:9)

I also know the gift has nothing to do with my own health. Some sceptics think that if one claims they can heal the sick, why are they suffering from health problems themselves. All the stories in this book are true and I write them while I am recovering from my second hip replacement. I have seen God give a man in Chile a new hip which was fantastic. All I know is God is the Creator and I am just one of His creatures. The rights I have as a Christian is the right to be called a son of God. John 1:12. We have the right of attorney to use the Lord Jesus' name when praying and blessing others. Everything else is in the bonus box.

And these signs shall follow them that believe; In my name shall they cast out devils; they shall speak with new tongues;

They shall take up serpents; and if they drink any deadly thing, it shall not hurt them; they shall lay hands on the sick, and they shall recover.

So then after the Lord had spoken unto them, he was received up into heaven, and sat on the right hand of God. (Mark 16:17-19)

CLOSE CALL

One day during my pastoral training I was asked to meet with a family in the evening to pray for their son who was in a coma. He had been riding his motorbike when a police car pulled out in front of him. He couldn't stop in time and the impact sent him over the top of the car. Unfortunately, he didn't have his helmet strapped on and it flew off. He hit the road landing on his head and from that time on he was in a coma. He had been that way for some weeks.

That evening I met the family at the hospital and talked with them before we went up to their son's ward. I said that because he is still alive, I am going to ask God to heal him and raise him up. If God doesn't do that, I want to pray a salvation prayer with him pausing during the prayer for him to repeat it in his mind. They agreed so we set off.

Roger (not his real name) was lying on his right side, he was covered in tattoos and appeared to me as if he had been living a hard life. I gathered he was quite likely their prodigal son. It was obvious the family loved him very much. I prayed for God to raise him up but He didn't. So, plan B was next. I prayed the salvation prayer pausing as if he was repeating it after me. I then said goodbye and left.

The next day we took nine of our youth group to Chile on a mission to the poor people around
Viña del Mar and were away for three weeks. On arriving home,

Close Call

I had a call from a lady in our church who was a friend of one of Roger's brothers. She sounded very excited on the phone and asked me if I had heard what happened to Roger. I said I hadn't heard anything. She then told me that the day after I visited Roger she went with the brother to pray in his ward.

After praying, his brother said he was worried that Roger might go to a lost eternity if he were to die. He said, "I need Roger to give me a sign that he accepted Christ as his Lord and Saviour."

They discussed what they should ask Roger to do as a sign. He said, "I want him to open his right eye." Now that was the eye that had never opened or moved during the whole time he had been in the coma. He then said, "I haven't got enough faith to ask him today. I will come back tomorrow."

When the brother went to see Roger the next day he asked, "If you received Jesus as your Saviour, I want you to open your right eye." His right eye was against the pillow and facing away from his brother. Roger opened his right eye. His brother also asked Roger to look at him. Roger turned his head right around and looked at him, and turned back. He then asked him to squeeze his other brother's hand who was sitting at his side. Roger squeezed his brother's hand and remained in the coma until a few days later when he passed away. God's amazing grace can reach into situations that we can't imagine or understand. What an amazing Saviour He is.

ICE CREAM TEST

We held a summer outreach at a beach north of Whangarei called Ngunguru. While there I held a healing meeting. At the meeting a lady brought her two sons forward for prayer. She told me that they both were allergic to dairy products. She had another boy the oldest one who also had the same problem who had gone, with his mum, to a Bill Subritzky meeting a year before and was healed. The other two boys didn't want to go at that time. This meant he had been eating ice creams for the last twelve months to the envy of his little brothers.

I prayed for the two boys to be healed from this allergy and then said to their mother, "There is one way to see if God has healed them and that is to buy them an ice cream."

She agreed and they all walked off to the local dairy. The next day I saw the mum and asked her how the ice cream test went. She said the boys had no reaction at all and were very happy campers.

KNOCKING ON HEAVEN'S DOOR

While out looking for carpet cleaning work I noticed an elderly man walking along the footpath when he suddenly stumbled. He didn't look too stable on his old walking stick.

I pulled my van to the side and jumped out running toward him, I said, "Are you okay?"

The old guy looked at me and said, "My heart's stuffed."

I thought to myself, "I might have to be quick here." I asked him if he knew Jesus as his personal Saviour.

He sort of craned his neck and looking down his nose said very assertively, "Yes I do."

I could see he was a bit shaken by me asking such a personal question. He was readying himself for a religious argument when I said, "You must be getting excited?"

He asked, "What do you mean?"

I then said, "You just told me your heart is stuffed and you know Jesus. Your heart could stop right now and you could be standing before the Lord."

He said, "I never thought of it like that."

I said, "That's what it's all about. And if it does happen, can you put in a good word for me?"

He looked at me and began to laugh. "I need to be around guys like you," and walked off home. I heard his heart quit on him not long after our meeting. I sometimes wonder if he got to put in a good word.

DIVINE APPOINTMENT

Pauline and I were driving back to the orphanage in Calapan City in the Philippines when our little Suzuki truck suddenly stopped. I tried starting it several times but to no avail. The truck had stalled right outside an auto-servicing shop. Pauline needed to get back to the office so we flagged a tricycle to take her back. I then went into the garage and asked if the mechanic could fix my truck. He said he would do it as soon as he finished his present job. The owner of the car he was working on was sitting waiting for his car to be ready. I sat down and introduced myself and we began to chat.

He asked me what I did in the Philippines and I told him I was a missionary and I was a Bible believing Christian. He said he was of a certain denomination and asked me if it was the same thing. Seizing the moment I was able to describe to him the differences between his religion and what Jesus taught in the scriptures and that they were very different. He wanted to know how to be born again so I explained how easy it was to do. Three things I told him:

1. Repent and realize that you are a sinner and you need forgiveness.
2. Believe Jesus died for your sins and rose again from the dead.
3. Receive Him into your life as your Lord and Saviour.

At this moment the mechanic finished his car and he was good to go. He said he would pray to God that night and do what I had

Divine Appointment

told him. I shook his hand and said goodbye. I went back to my truck to see if I would need to push it into the garage. I tried the ignition, just in case, and the motor burst into life. I explained to the mechanic I didn't seem to need his help and drove off back to the base, thanking God for His ability to arrange circumstances.

FALSE IMPRESSION

While on outreach in Mexico we travelled to a very poor province where we stayed in a local YWAM base. On the Sunday morning I was to preach at the morning service in a little church a few miles away. The service started at 7:00 am. These amigos were really keen to hear the word of God.

They were all elderly and had walked for sixteen hours sleeping overnight in the fields then travelling on to church. After the sermon I prayed for a lady who had poor eyesight. She came forward and I asked her if she could read the big letters of the church's motto over the altar. She could not read them so I prayed for her and asked her if she could now read them. She still couldn't read them. She went back to her seat and sat down. I then asked for those with sore backs to come forward. Many of these elderly men had bad backs because of their hard-working lives. I was half way along the line and God healed each one when all of a sudden, the lady with poor sight jumped up and began praising the Lord. She could see perfectly and was so happy.

After the service we went out back to have breakfast. I was sitting beside a young Mexican guy and opposite the bus driver, a rugged looking amigo. I noticed that his eyes were welling with tears and I thought to myself he must have been moved by my sermon. I looked at the young guy beside me and he too had tears streaming down his cheeks. I was now quite chuffed that my preaching had cut so deep into their hearts. It was at that point I noticed each one was holding a half-eaten chili and were having a 'chili off.' Mexicans love to prove their manhood by seeing if they can eat more chilies than their opposition. Their chilies are super-hot. All of my self-adulation went right out the window very quickly.

COVEN VERSES COVENANT

During an outreach on the outskirts of Mexico City we set up our sound system in a local park. As we were setting-up we noticed a group of young people down the far end of the park dressed in black coats. One of the locals told us they were Darks, another word for Satanists. I decided to seize the moment and went, over to the group, with a local guy to invite them to our presentation. As we came closer I could see that these guys were pretty serious about whatever it was they were in to. They had painted red lines down their eyelids some had white painted faces.

I said, "Would you like to come to our show ballet, drama etc?" We then left and went back to our group.

Our presentation consisted of a jazz dance to some catchy music. Our team had practised for weeks during the Bible study part of our course and they were pretty good. This was followed by a short testimony from one of the team about their overcoming drug addiction or a sad childhood etc. Then followed the main act; A drama of the creation right through to Jesus' death and resurrection performed to the music theme of Mission Impossible. One of the team had to play the part of the devil and he had a very scary mask that really was effective.

The show went well and we were just starting the main drama when I noticed the Satanists coming toward the crowd. They all sat down and began to watch. I was thinking this is great when all of a sudden my world was turned upside down. Our Satan came bursting onto the scene to carry out his deceiving part of the act and the Satanists all gave a loud cheer. "Oh no," I thought, "this is not good." Every time the Devil came out the Satanists would cheer. I was not prepared for this kind of reaction and thought they had ruined our chances of seeing any salvations that day.

However, God had other plans. When the drama had finished we noticed there was uneasiness, in the group of Satanists, because the leader's girlfriend had started to sob her heart out. No matter what they did they couldn't get her to stop crying. They realized there was a power in their presence far greater than what they had been messing with. They carried her back to the other end of the park with our team in hot pursuit. The team carried on talking with them about Jesus and I went down with a local pastor to keep an eye on proceedings to make sure our team was safe. After a while I felt it was time to leave, but before we left the pastor asked the two leaders to meet him and another pastor the next day for coffee. They agreed and we went back to pack up and climb on the bus and leave for the next town.

Two days later we received an email telling us what happened with the Satanists after we left.

The two coven leaders met with the pastors for coffee and received the Lord as their Saviour. They decided that the coven would join the church's youth group. I have been a strong believer in drama ever since.

MY EXPERIENCE IN A MEXICAN PRISON

While on our outreach tour of Mexico we had the opportunity to visit a Mexican prison way out in the desert somewhere. We arrived and went through all the security checks and gates until we arrived at the exercise yard of this security prison. Our team set up the sound system and prepared themselves for their routines and drama. Some were a bit nervous which was quite understandable. Seated around the perimeter of the yard were prisoners wondering what was going on. Some of them were obviously hardened criminals, some sat on chairs and others on the ground waiting to see what these gringos had brought to entertain their boring lives.

The interpreter introduced the team and they began with their jazz dance then a small drama about drug addiction. Then we had the main drama which went off without a hitch. I preached a gospel message and when I had finished God gave me the impression that there was a person there that had a sore back. Actually it was more at the top of the right buttock cheek. I placed my thumb there to demonstrate where the pain was in the person I believed had the problem. It sure was a test of my ability to hear correctly what the Holy Spirit was saying to me. After the interpreter explained what I had said and where the pain was there was a dead silence. I thought to myself, this is not a good place to be practicing whether or not I am actually hearing from the Lord. The prisoner's faces seemed to be more unfriendly towards me than they did before as the uninterrupted silence seemed to drag on forever. As I was eying up the exit gate, and rapidly counting the number of steps it would take me to reach it, a man stood up and started walking towards me. He came and stood in front of me and said he had pain in that part of his backside.

I prayed for him and he was instantly released of the pain and I then got the interpreter to ask him what had caused the pain. He said that he had been shot and the bullet was never removed but now all the pain was gone. That was a moment to be so grateful to God and the visit to that prison ended on a high note. God showed them He loves and cares about them and their eternal state even in prison miles from anywhere.

GOD'S IN THE ROOM

Some wonderful friends of ours rang with some bad news. Their son who had been a Christian but had walked away from the faith, was in the process of coming back to God, and had suffered a terrible car accident. His car had left the road and slammed into a tree. He was in a coma in the local hospital and they wanted Pauline and me to go and pray for him. On arriving at the hospital, we met up with his girlfriend and her friend and his girlfriend's mother. The two girls escorted us to his room while the mother stayed behind. As we entered his body began to twitch violently. I thought to myself the spirit of death does not want us here. He seemed very agitated. We walked over to the bed and I began to talk to him knowing he could hear me in his spirit. I asked God to heal him and raise him up off the bed, but that was not to be. I began to lead him to the Lord in a prayer pausing to let him repeat it in his spirit.

All of a sudden, an incredible peace came over his body as I said the prayer. The two girls sensed the presence of God, freaking out they took off down the corridor yelling, "God's in the room, God's in the room."

The presence and peace of God was so intense in the room, I could never forget that amazing experience. Sadly, he never came out of the coma, and died soon after. We were able to tell the parents what had happened which brought them such reassurance. The funeral was an amazing celebration of the young man's life and the parents were such an example to everyone, of the hope and strength that comes from knowing God and the saving power through His Son.

TANTALIZING OTHERS WITH YOUR TESTIMONY

I was having a new windscreen put in my car and after filling in time wandering around the town, I thought I would check up on the progress on my car. I was whistling an old Bill Black tune from the fifties as I arrived at the garage.

The young guy working on my car said, "You're a happy fellow."

I quickly replied, "Yep, I am going to heaven and I am glad about that!" I then began to ask him all about his job and how he fixed chips on windscreens etc.

I could see this was beginning to stir his curiosity, I think he was thinking, "How can he say such a random thing and then not say anything else?"

I walked over to the other mechanic and started chatting to him. He asked me what I did. I said, "I was a missionary in the Philippines."

This was too much for the young mechanic and he stopped what he was doing and came over to join the conversation. "What is it that you do in the Philippines?"

I began to tell these two mechanics that I taught the Bible under trees or where ever, planted churches and such. Then I switched my story to a recent testimony from a few days prior.

I said, "I was talking to this chap the other day over a coffee while we discussed the plans for a small dwelling I wanted built on our property. I handed him my card and he noticed from the card I was a Christian. He said, 'So you are a Christian?' I said, 'For sure' (always answer that question knowing that anyone who isn't, is missing out). I told him Christians don't believe some pie in the sky kind of thing. We can prove our faith. He looked kind of curious and asked, 'How can you do that?' I said, 'We have a court case. First, we put Jesus' resurrection on the stand and then we ask for eye witnesses to give their side of the story. Then Jesus' disciples all came in and they all said the same thing. They all swore they had seen Jesus alive after his crucifixion. Now here's the interesting thing,' I told him. 'Most of them died horrific deaths believing that they knew Jesus was alive. Not one denied it. So why would they die for a lie?' The chap looked at me and said to me, 'Yeah, why would they die for a lie?'"

As they had heard my testimony these two mechanics looked at each other and said to each other, "Yeah, why would they die for a lie?"

Testimony is powerful and every Christian has a testimony. What we forget to do is to begin to collect them. When you first become a Christian, you have a testimony. When you tell somebody about how you became a Christian, take note of how they reacted to your story. Now you have another testimony. All you have to do is keep telling people about your own testimonies, about your life as a follower of Christ, and next thing you have a collection of testimonies to draw from for all kinds of situations. Because they are your stories no one can argue with them and you become more and more naturally spiritual and spiritually natural. May the Lord bless you as you spread the wonderful news of Christ with the others in your life.

CONCLUSION

I hope you have enjoyed my testimonies. I can assure you that living life knowing that God has your back allows you to seize the moment when it comes to sharing your faith. I have been a missionary since 2001 having spent most of that time in the Philippines directing Mercy Link. The ministry was involved with bible studies, medical outreaches and dental outreaches on the Island of Mindoro. For the last four years I have helped my wife with the orphanage she established on the island.

On one of our medical outreaches in 2005 we found a little tribal Mangyan boy who was starving and severely malnourished. He was the second child to come into our care. When I first saw him, I was shocked at his physical and emotional condition. His skin was peeling off in places, his hair was falling out, his eyes were glazed, his ribs were sticking out and he had the pot tummy of a malnourished child. His little neck was so thin it seemed impossible for it to hold up the weight of his head. I thought that he would not last a week. I chose in my mind not to get too attached to little Ryan because I was sure he would soon die.

One evening Pauline said that Ryan had the cutest giggle.

I said, "How come?"

She said she had him in our room and sat him on the bed and made a funny face and a funny noise and he began to giggle. I couldn't believe what she was telling me could be true. The next morning she brought him in to our room and put him on the bed beside me and pulled a funny face and that was it. I heard the most amazing little chuckle from this little wrinkled up boy and from that moment on I was totally attached.

This little man who looked like an old man in a baby's body soon began to improve and a few weeks later he turned into the cutest, healthy baby. The cutest little brown two year old I had ever seen. His own mum had died from TB and he decided Pauline would be his new mum. He wanted to be with her so badly that he would sit at the top of the stairs at the orphanage and call out continuously, "Mama, mama your house."

The only way she could get any work done was to put him by her desk with some toys. As long as he was around Mama everything was okay in his world. After a few weeks he had worn Mama out and Mama gave in to his demands and he got to stay in Mama's house and is now our very own adopted son. Pauline and I couldn't be more proud of our son who is now a fine young man.

Pauline's orphanage and ministry is called Ruel Foundation 'Give a Smile'. I am now working on my retirement which seems to be eluding me. We have a small orchard and lots of grass to mow, trees to prune etc.

I take my music to retirement villages and get heaps of joy out of singing and playing for the elderly in all the different villages. All things are possible in God as one day I played my Nanna's favourite hymn 'How Great Thou Art' and some ended up worshipping God, hands held high in the middle of the main lounge during happy hour.

God has kept His word that life for me following Him will be an abundant life. (John 10:10)

Seizing the Moment

Don't strive, let God drive and you will have a life of wonderful moments and opportunities. May God the Father and Jesus Christ His only begotten Son fill you with the Holy Spirit to help you seize the moment that is waiting for you to happen.

If you have never believed in Jesus Christ but now would like to become a Christian, why not seize this moment, it may be the only one you get to make such an important choice, and follow the prayer.

SALVATION PRAYER

It is not the prayer that saves you but rather the attitude of your heart. Jesus is the only one who can save your soul and bring you into His incredible salvation (eternal inheritance). This prayer is to help you claim by faith the steps that are found in the Bible to be saved by God's grace through faith. When you pray, talk to God as you would a friend you know you can totally trust. Pray with sincerity and respect realizing that He is awesome.

Prayer
Heavenly Father I know that I have sinned in my life and realize I need a Saviour. I am sorry for my sins and ask You to forgive me.

I believe that Your Son Jesus died on the cross for my sins and that His unique blood can cleanse me from *all* of my sin.

I believe that He rose again after the third day from the grave and is now seated beside You in heaven.

I ask You Jesus to be the Lord of my life, and I invite You to dwell in me by your Holy Spirit.

I receive You now by faith and ask You to help me to be your disciple, and to give me courage to tell others about You.

Thank you for saving me and cleansing me from all my sin and taking me from a hopeless end to an endless hope.

I pray this prayer in the name of Jesus Christ. Amen

If you feel like telling me of your salvation you can email me.
I would be thrilled to hear from you regardless.
wkcurtissmith@gmail.com

www.ingramcontent.com/pod-product-compliance
Lightning Source LLC
Chambersburg PA
CBHW070303010526
44108CB00039B/1699